# SHARING SPACES

## TIPS AND STRATEGIES ON BEING A GOOD COLLEGE ROOMMATE, SURVIVING A BAD ONE, AND DEALING WITH EVERYTHING IN BETWEEN

### BY HEATHER ALEXANDER

KAPLAN

**Simon & Schuster**
**New York ◉ London ◉ Tokyo ◉ Sydney**

Kaplan Publishing
Published by Simon & Schuster, Inc.
1230 Avenue of the Americas
New York, NY 10020

For information regarding special discounts for bulk purchases, please contact Simon & Schuster Special Sales at 1-800-456-6798 or business@simonandschuster.com.

Cover Design: Bradford Foltz
Interior Design: Heather Kern
Cover Illustration: Kim Johnson
Editor: Helena Santini

Manufactured in the United States of America

July 2004

10 9 8 7 6 5 4 3 2 1

Library of Congress Cataloging-in-Publication Data

ISBN: 0-7432-6151-8

# ACKNOWLEDGMENTS

To "Joe"—my then-and-forever roommate—and to the girls of 224 Eddy, who showed me the joy of having college roommates who become great friends.

Special thanks to Helena Santini for all her guidance and great ideas.

# CONTENTS

## WANTED:

College roommate who is fun (but not too rowdy),
clean (but not obsessive-compulsive),
quiet (but not boring), and super-friendly.

Must share my taste in music, have no bodily odors, and be
willing to let me borrow anything I want. Those who might
talk about me behind my back, snore, hang out in our room
all the time, go through my stuff, and/or make a move on my
significant other NEED NOT APPLY.

**D**reaming of that perfect college roommate? Join the club.

Every August, millions of students flood college campuses, facing a tidal wave of new classes, new schedules, and new experiences. But sometimes, the biggest pressure of all is The New Roommate.

After all, whether you're a first-day freshman or a fourth-year senior, how you interact with your roommate will affect your college experience as much as all the late nights in the computer center, the romantic hookups, and the new friends you'll make combined! In the year ahead, you will be sharing private moments, pre-exam stress, and just about everything else with this person—whether you want to or not. Will your roommate turn out to be a pleasure to live with, or the nightmare that you just can't seem to wake up from?

Rest assured <u>everyone</u> has roommate issues—from borrowing clothes to borrowing boyfriends, from late-night parties to late-night snoring, from splitting the phone bill to dividing the room down the middle. But have no fear. This book is packed with quotes and advice from college students and recent grads who have been through it all—and want to make the experience easier for you.

These pages hold tales from the tormented, funny stories and solutions, and the secrets to getting along. Living with another person is an incredible opportunity to learn—both about other people and about yourself, and this book can help you get the most out of your roommate experience.

Ready for Roommate 101? Then turn the page for the real-deal answers to all your roommate questions!

# 1

# A MATCH MADE IN HEAVEN?

*My college roommate is still my best friend in the world. We're like sisters.*

ANTHROPOLOGY/SOCIOLOGY MAJOR, URSINUS COLLEGE

*My college roommate was Satan!*

ENVIRONMENTAL SCIENCE MAJOR, EMORY UNIVERSITY

# Choosing a college roommate is like a game of Roomie Roulette.

The great, big wheel is spun around and around. As it slows, you cross your fingers. Will it land on complete incompatibility or instant soul mate? Welcome to round one of the roommate game! In some cases, you choose the roommate. In other cases, the roommate is chosen for you. Either way, you're going to have to adjust to a whole new way of life with this person.

  One way to make this transition easier is to work out some issues with your roommate before school even begins. This chapter will show you how to get your relationship started.

**I**t's spring of your senior year in high school. You've just mailed in your acceptance forms—you're off to college! Then the big packet arrives. It's stuffed with official-looking documents, one of which is most likely the ROOMMATE QUESTIONNAIRE.

Most colleges' or universities' housing departments give incoming freshmen questionnaires to match up compatible roommates. Some schools ask a few general questions about your living and studying habits; others probe deeper with a multitude of questions, right down to your choice of breakfast cereal. Whatever the case, this is not the time to show off your creative-writing skills. See below for a list of helpful hints to follow when filling out these forms.

1. **Don't lie.** If you are messy, admit it. If you like to wake up at three o'clock in the afternoon on weekends, admit it. No matter what you <u>desire</u> to be, your true self will soon be apparent to your new roomie. Don't think that a roommate who is clean will get you to be a cleaner person, because all it will get you is a roommate who is resentful of your messy ways. And p.s.—even if you're "trying to cut back," don't check the box that says "non-smoker." Otherwise, it's a safe bet that you will be forced by your non-smoking roommate to stand outside in the freezing cold to have a cigarette.

2. **Fill out the form yourself.** Face it—if your parents fill out the form, they would never write down that you like to party or plan on pulling an all-nighter. Is your goal really to end up with a roommate that's a perfect match for Mom and Dad?

3. **Be honest with yourself.** College is a wonderful opportunity to meet students from completely different backgrounds. But while an obsessive-compulsive neat-freak and a slob who never changes his sheets can easily get along as friends, would they make the best roommates? How willing are you to live with lifestyles so different from your own? Indicate the truth on the questionnaire.

FAMOUS
Al Gore and Tommy Lee Jones
ROOMIES

# STUDENTS SAY:
## THE TRUTH IS IN THE PROSE (KIND OF)

I just wish that I had filled out the application that requests your roommate preferences. My mom decided that it would be a good influence on me to have a roommate from a "farm community."

**COMPUTER SCIENCE MAJOR, SEATTLE UNIVERSITY**

I had talked to my roommate on the phone before college. She told me what she had written on the housing form. It turns out her answers weren't rooted in truth. I left for college thinking we'd be compatible, and I spent the entire year feeling lied to.

**INTEGRATED MARKETING COMMUNICATIONS MAJOR, EMERSON COLLEGE**

*I'm from a big city on the east coast and when I found out my roommate was from a rural town in a state halfway across the country, I wondered why I even took the time to fill out the questionnaire in the first place—clearly they hadn't done a good job! But even though our backgrounds were different, our living styles were perfectly compatible, and I kept the same roommate for four years!*

**ARTS ADMINISTRATION MAJOR, WAGNER COLLEGE**

# Cyber Roommates

Many universities are using the Internet to pair students. The colleges send incoming freshmen to specific websites, where they can scroll through profiles and pictures of potential roomies and contact possible matches.

The colleges and universities who are currently using this method feel it gives the student more control in the roommate process. Other colleges feel that online matching inflates expectations of having found the perfect roommate and thus increases disappointment when everyday conflicts arise.

What do you think?

**A**fter answering all the questions on the questionnaire, it might seem like a better plan to just room with someone you know (if you have that option). But is that always the right thing to do? Check out the list below—living with a stranger might be too good to pass up!

## PROS TO LIVING WITH A STRANGER:

- He won't remember the fashion-challenged haircut you had in the ninth grade.

- She may broaden your world, exposing you to new and interesting cultures.

- Students often find it easier to tell someone who is not their friend if something is bothering them about the living situation. If you're living with a friend, you often let more things slide—but that doesn't mean those things don't get on your nerves.

- Living with someone is an important part of learning how to cope on your own in a new situation—skills you will need later in life.

- You'll have the possibility of making a new friend!

# STUDENTS SAY: STRANGER IS THE WAY TO GO

You have nothing to lose by rooming with a stranger, and only an awesome experience to gain.

POLITICAL SCIENCE MAJOR, TEXAS TECH UNIVERSITY—LUBBOCK

I think going into a living situation with three people in a small room was better because of the fact that none of us knew each other prior to move-in day. We were more respectful than we might have been had we been closer. And since we evolved together from strangers to best friends, we kept the mutual respect for a long time.

SOCIOLOGY MAJOR, PENNSYLVANIA STATE UNIVERSITY

*Despite the fact that my roommate and I had very little in common when we first met, we got along and remained friends throughout college. I'm glad I was thrown together with her, because otherwise I'm sure we would have never met by ourselves on campus.*

CRIMINAL JUSTICE MAJOR, GEORGE WASHINGTON UNIVERSITY

**Okay, so we told you all the good things about living with a stranger,** but you're still not taking any chances. You're determined to live with a friend! Sure, there are tons of instances where friends live together and have a great time. But we just want to leave you with a few questions to ask yourself before you decide for sure:

➤ You have never lived in a 18' x 18' room for an entire year with your friend. Do you think you can stand being with him that up-close and personal 24/7? Sometimes living with someone makes you learn more about him than you ever wanted to know.

➤ Does your friend have habits that annoy you? If so, multiply the annoyance factor by 365, because you will be living with that habit every day.

➤ Just because you used to pal around in high school, do you have the same goals in terms of grades, schoolwork, and social life? Will your friend be able to accept if you want different things out of your college experience or want to make new friends? Will you be able to handle it if it happens to you?

➡ Will it be harder for you to make new friends if you live with your friend? Will you use your friend or will she use you as a crutch and, as a result, not venture out to meet new people?

➡ Do you want your friend telling everyone back in your hometown what you are up to on campus? If not, can your college life really stay at college while living with your friend?

# STUDENTS SAY: FRIEND ≠ GOOD ROOMMATE

I wish I had roomed with someone I did not know. I roomed with my best friend, and we were on each other's back the entire year. It almost ruined our friendship.

CRIMINOLOGY MAJOR, MARQUETTE UNIVERSITY

My freshman roommate was my best friend from home. DO NOT DO IT. Even though I already knew her, my impression of her changed when I lived with her. She was much less considerate and much sloppier than I had realized. Living with someone is very different than just being friends.

LAW MAJOR, ALBANY LAW SCHOOL

My freshman roommate and I had gone to boarding school together. Unfortunately, living together was easy within the confines of a boarding school because we had rules to follow that we did not have in college. I learned that you must have a clear idea of _how_ you are going to live together in order for the situation to work.

HISTORY/ENGLISH MAJOR, McGILL UNIVERSITY

People change so much between the summer before college and the summer after that even if you knew the person well prior to living with him, he'll probably be a different person by the end of the year.

JOURNALISM/POLITICS MAJOR, NEW YORK UNIVERSITY

My roommate and I didn't know each other that well, but our mothers were friends. I was a bit of a wild child my freshman year. She told her mother, who told my mother, and my mother ended up knowing more about my freshman year than she needed to know!

PHILOSOPHY MAJOR, HAMLINE UNIVERSITY

# STUDENTS SAY: STICK BY YOUR FRIENDS

*It's easy to live with someone who is your good friend—all is fair game, anything can be said, and not as many compromises are necessary because you already have a bond based on more than just sharing a room.*

**COMPUTER SCIENCE MAJOR, GEORGE WASHINGTON UNIVERSITY**

**Don't listen to people who tell you not to room with a friend. My freshman roommate was a stranger, we didn't have anything in common, and as a result, we didn't get along. After that I lived with friends and it was a great experience because we shared common ground.**

**BUSINESS MAJOR, UNIVERSITY OF TEXAS—AUSTIN**

Don't believe the myth that if you live with your best friend, you will end up hating each other, because it is not true. If your personalities are compatible, you will be fine.

**PSYCHOLOGY MAJOR, UNIVERSITY OF MISSOURI**

## A WORD TO THE WISE:

If you can't decide whether or not you should live with your friend, there is a compromise to be made. Opt to live in the same dorm or even on the same hall. Here's why students say this works:

- ☐ Instantly, your opportunity to make new friends doubles. You get to meet his friends; he gets to meet yours.

- ☐ You get the security of living near someone who likes and trusts you, yet you don't have to spend every minute with her.

- ☐ If your roommate bugs you or you suddenly feel homesick, you can just go down the hall to vent or see a familiar face.

- ☐ You will also have the choice open to you: to stay friends or not.

**P**icture it: It's the first day of college and you are surrounded by your parents, a mountain of suitcases, and a whiny little brother. This is <u>not</u> how you want to meet your roommate for the first time!

Luckily, most colleges will reveal the name, address, email address, and phone number of your future roommate a month or two before you move in. All college students offer the same advice: <u>get in touch before move-in day</u>. Why? Because it gives you a chance to uncover what the person you'll be living with for the next year is <u>really</u> like. It will also help you find some common ground so that your first face-to-face meeting will be less stressful. Here are some getting-to-know-you questions to ask your roommate that might give you some insight into her living style:

1. **"What are your expectations for school?"** If your roommate answers, "to get straight A's" you'll know you're probably not dealing with someone from the cast of *Animal House*. If your roommate answers, "to party like it's 1999," don't plan on many quiet evenings!

2. **"What is your favorite food?"** If he answers, "steamed tofu and brown rice," you're probably headed for disapproving glares when you bring fast-food burgers back to the room. If he answers, "gummy fish, potato chips, and chocolate," your fridge is probably going to be junk-food central.

3.  **"How do you like to de-stress?"** If she answers, "go for a ten-mile run every morning at dawn," you know you've got a healthy, early-bird roommate. If she answers, "chug beers at the bars until I can't see straight," expect potential late-night puke-fests in your room.

4.  **"If you could be stranded on a deserted island with only one person, who would it be?"** If he answers "My girlfriend . . . and she goes to our school,"  don't plan on hanging with your roommate much—or plan on hanging out with his girlfriend a lot! If he answers, "my mommy," it's a pretty safe bet that there will be many homesick nights in your room.

5.  **"What are your interests?"** If she answers "shopping for shoes and handbags," realize that closet space will be at a premium. If she answers "hot-wiring cars," find your RA—and quick!

# Top 5 Things You Hope Your Roommate Doesn't Say on the Phone:

5. I have a bed-wetting problem. Do you still want me to take the top bunk?

4. My hamsters get claustrophobic in their cage. They need to wander around the room during the day.

3. I'm in training for the Nathan's hot dog eating contest.

2. Once a month, three Colombian men will be stopping by to deliver packages.

1. I have my own website. Everything we do will be broadcast live on the Internet!

## STUDENTS SAY: GET IN TOUCH

I wished I had talked to my roommate beforehand. We both entered the situation assuming we had the same expectations of each other—but we definitely didn't! Just one little conversation would have helped a lot.

AMERICAN STUDIES MAJOR, UNIVERSITY OF TEXAS—AUSTIN

**We talked for weeks before school started, so I already felt like we were friends before we even got there.**

POLITICAL SCIENCE MAJOR, WESTMONT COLLEGE

*Talk about guidelines early on. It only gets harder later.*

FOOD SCIENCE MAJOR, UNIVERSITY OF FLORIDA—GAINESVILLE

*It helped my roommate and me to ask a lot of "getting to know you" questions that had nothing to do with our living arrangements. This helped to ease the awkwardness of the move-in because we had an increased comfort level. We also swapped pictures, so when we finally met it felt like we knew each other a little bit.*

ENGLISH LITERATURE MAJOR, COLORADO COLLEGE

**We discussed the issues that were important to us on the phone. We developed a mutual respect and trust for each other by doing this.**

COMMUNICATION STUDIES MAJOR, FLORIDA STATE UNIVERSITY

# DO YOUR HOMEWORK: ISSUES TO RESOLVE BEFORE YOU GET THERE

**Y**ou're on the phone or in the middle of emailing your new roommate. You've talked about your interests, the names of your dogs, where you partied after your senior prom—now what? It's time to get down to business: who brings what. Here's a list of common shared items that students often forget about bringing to school. Go over this list with your roommate and decide what each person is going to bring.

**Colander** (a necessity when making Mac 'n Cheese)
**Plastic container** (for mixing powdered drink mixes)
**Clothes drying rack**
**Message board for your door**
**Fan** (if there is no air conditioning in your dorm, make it a BIG fan!)
**"Fun Tack" to hang things on walls** (most schools don't allow nails or tape)
**Booklight** (so you don't keep your roomie awake when you want to read in bed and vice versa)
**Flashlight and extra batteries**
**Power strip**
**Cleaning supplies**
**Extension cords**
**Sleeping bag or extra blankets** (you never know who may spend the night)

Adapted from: "What to Bring." www.aboutcollege.com/whattobring.htm

I wish we had discussed what types of kitchenware we would be bringing. This may seem like a small item, but you try eating cereal with a fork!

PHILOSOPHY MAJOR, UNIVERSITY OF GEORGIA

## We didn't discuss what to bring—and ended up with two TVs, two bath mats, two sets of dishes . . . basically two of everything!

INTERNATIONAL BUSINESS AND MARKETING MAJOR, GEORGE WASHINGTON UNIVERSITY

*I wish we discussed sharing a fridge. I wanted one and I thought she'd want one too. I was surprised when we got to school and she said she didn't need one.*

JOURNALISM MAJOR, PEPPERDINE UNIVERSITY

We should have talked about not only what we were bringing, but how much. It would have been easier not having so much stuff cluttering up our room.

SPANISH/HISTORY MAJOR, WILLAMETTE UNIVERSITY

I wish I knew he was going to invade our small fridge with a 30-pack of beer the first day—I didn't have any room for my mother's home-cooked food!

ENGLISH MAJOR, UNIVERSITY OF WISCONSIN—MADISON

## So you've had a few interactions with your new roommate, and you think you know what you're in for come moving day.

But are you really? There's a lot to be accomplished in that first week at school, so read on to make sure you know the issues you'll be up against and how to handle them!

# 2 MEETING AND GREETING

*The first day I met my roommate, he was drunk. I told myself that first impressions don't count. But then he stayed drunk for the whole two years that I lived with him!*

MARKETING MAJOR, UNIVERSITY OF ALABAMA

# You've arrived at college. You're about to meet your roommate face-to-face.

What happens in the next week could lay the groundwork for the entire year. You don't want to mess that up, right?

There's a lot to accomplish: You'll have to get to know the person you are living with, set up and decorate your shoebox of a room, and completely adjust to a new way of life. No need for panic—having a roommate is going to be fun if you handle it the right way, and this chapter will help get you started!

# FIRST IMPRESSIONS: LOOKS CAN BE DECEIVING

**There are many common misconceptions** that roommates have when they go into a new living situation. Check out the ones that students brought up the most—and if you find yourself in one of these situations, remember not to prejudge!

## At first I thought my roommate was . . .

nice and a little on the quiet side. She turned out to be completely wild.

GERMANIC LANGUAGES AND LITERATURE MAJOR, WASHINGTON UNIVERSITY—ST. LOUIS

smart and brash. Actually, he was more sensitive and complex than I had previously supposed.

ENGLISH MAJOR, UNIVERSITY OF CALIFORNIA—DAVIS

*a bumpkin from the hills of Montana. Actually, she was very smart, interesting, and metropolitan.*

LAW MAJOR, UNIVERSITY OF MICHIGAN

a real snob. Turns out that she was just incredibly shy. She ended up being one of my best friends.

BUSINESS MAJOR, GEORGE WASHINGTON UNIVERSITY

## STUDENTS SAY: LOOK BEYOND

I misjudged my roommate due to the fact that her overbearing mother was with us when we first met.

GEOGRAPHY MAJOR, QUEEN'S UNIVERSITY

If there is one thing I learned in college, it is that some people simply take longer to warm up than others . . . and it is usually worth the wait.

SPANISH LITERATURE MAJOR, WASHINGTON UNIVERSITY—ST. LOUIS

*First impressions are just that—impressions, not how a person really is. You need to take time to sit and talk with a new roommate and find out about her likes and dislikes and past history to really know who she is.*

BIOLOGY MAJOR, UNIVERSITY OF SOUTH FLORIDA

## STUDENTS SAY: THE SNAP JUDGMENT

Of course there are always a <u>few</u> instances where first impressions are accurate. Like these for example . . .

He sounded like a nerd over the phone, and he was a nerd in person. My friends joked that when I met him, he would have a calculator watch. Sure enough, he had a calculator watch!

**BUSINESS MAJOR, UNIVERSITY OF TEXAS—AUSTIN**

# Nice and dumb—and she was, in fact, nice and dumb.

**PUBLIC RELATIONS MAJOR, UNIVERSITY OF HOUSTON**

I thought she was sweet, smart, funny, and kind. I was so right. She was the best roommate in roommate history.

**LITERARY AND CULTURAL STUDIES MAJOR, UNIVERSITY OF OKLAHOMA**

# DIVIDE AND CONQUER

**T**he first potential problem you could have with your roommate is deciding who gets what furniture in the room and where the furniture should go. When you first set foot in your dorm room you'll find yourself in one of three situations:

1. **You're the first one there.** Time to grab all the best stuff, right? Rein it in a second, partner. You want to be fair to your roommate. And that means:

   ★ **Wait until your roommate arrives.** We know you want to get unpacked and start enjoying college life, but stop and think about the situation from your new roomie's point of view. What if you arrived second and were left with only one drawer and the worst bed? Do unto your roommate as you would want done unto you.

   ★ **Make a plan.** Survey the room. Decide what you think is the best way to divide everything evenly. This way when your roommate arrives, you can present her with a clear plan that she can then react to. If your roommate isn't scheduled to arrive until the next day, make sure you discuss the issue in advance.

2.  **Your roommate is already there and is in the middle of taking the bigger closet and the nicer desk for herself.** Before you go psycho on her, do the following:

    ★ **Take a deep breath.** Count to ten or twenty or whatever number it takes to calm down and assess the situation.

    ★ **Talk to your roommate.** Tell her (calmly!) that you see she has claimed the biggest closet, so you feel it is only fair that you get the nicer desk.

3. **Your roomie is all set up, has taken everything you wanted, and is probably catching the 4–4:30 welcome lunch in the dining hall.** Instead of seething over this for the rest of the year or tossing his clothes into the hall, why not try the following instead?

★ **Sit tight until he returns.** Calmly point out that while you appreciate how organized and industrious he has been in setting up the room, he left you no choices.

★ **Meet halfway.** Make some compromises. Say that since he has already unpacked his clothes into the nicer dresser, you would like to switch beds with him. Or if it is the closet that is really important to you, offer to help him move his clothes into the other closet.

★ **Assert yourself.** You have every right to be part of the decision-making process in your own room. If your roommate won't budge, insisting that the early bird catches the worm, control your temper and take a nice stroll down to your RA's room. (Hey, you had to meet him sooner or later!) One of the RA's jobs is to help resolve roommate conflicts—this qualifies.

## STUDENTS SAY: WHO GETS WHAT AND WHAT GOES WHERE_

My roommate really wanted the bed next to the window. Even though I wanted it, I gave it to her. Turns out she got cold every night in the winter and I didn't!

LAW MAJOR, STATE UNIVERSITY OF NEW YORK—ALBANY

I wish we had discussed our preferences ahead of time. My roommate got to school first and left me the lower bunk bed because she thought I'd prefer it, although in reality she really wanted to sleep there. I would have rather had the top bunk but didn't say anything because I thought she wanted it!

PERFORMANCE STUDIES MAJOR, NORTHWESTERN UNIVERSITY

*When I first walked into my dorm room, my roommate was already there and she and her parents had set it up with the beds bunked. I am an only child and I could not deal with the thought of sleeping above or below someone else—I need my own space. Together we figured out a way to arrange our room so there were no bunk beds but enough room for all our stuff.*

PHILOSOPHY MAJOR, HAMLINE UNIVERSITY

**We compromised on space issues.** She had more shelves on her side of the room, so I ended up getting slightly more floor space.

ETHICS MAJOR, YALE UNIVERSITY

**H**ome, sweet, home! A shoebox-sized room with drab cinder block walls, a closet with no door, and metal bunk beds— sounds cozy, doesn't it?

Even the most interior decorating-challenged students would never leave the room this way. In this age of home-improvement TV shows, every student has a shot of converting his barracks-like dorm room into a warm, inviting place that doesn't seem divided down the middle, but instead, seems like one room. Here are some simple steps to get you and your roomie started on your dorm room décor:

◘ **Light It Up:** String holiday lights all the way around the room—no matter what time of year, they always bring cheer. Or buy scented candles. They'll make the room smell nice and give a warm glow to the harsh dorm lighting.

◘ **The Walls Say It All:** Buy several matching bulletin boards or ribbon boards and each of you cover them with photos of your family, pets, and hometown friends. Or try hanging a tapestry with colors or a pattern that you both like. Buy stencils at a craft store and stencil a border around the room.

◘ **Don't Pull the Rug Out:** Plan to buy a rug for your room that matches both your comforters. Carpets reduce noise and give the room warmth. Avoid white or light-colored rugs, so you won't be blamed for the muddy boot prints.

## A WORD TO THE WISE:

Before you and your roommate go shopping together, take measurements. Otherwise, you may haul a futon up three flights of stairs only to find out that it's a foot too long.

▣ **Store It:** You and your roommate will need to make the most of what little space you have. Plastic stackable drawers are great for extra sweaters and sweatshirts. Portable file boxes will help keep the clutter off your desk. And don't overlook all that space under your bed. Raise your beds by putting a brick under each leg and buy storage boxes for seldom-used clothes and extra linens and blankets that you can store underneath.

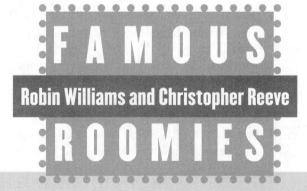

FAMOUS

Robin Williams and Christopher Reeve

ROOMIES

This is what happened to the students who <u>didn't</u> discuss decorating issues with their roommates—don't wind up like them!

It's a bad idea to go to school with no interior decorating plans. Our dorm room was bare for an entire semester!

FINANCE MAJOR, UNIVERSITY OF NOTRE DAME

I wish I had known before school started that my roommate was obsessed with *Star Wars* and felt compelled to put Yoda posters all over our room.

ENVIRONMENTAL POLICY MAJOR, RUTGERS UNIVERSITY

*One day when I was out, my roommate moved all of our furniture around. I couldn't find any of my things!*

TELECOMMUNICATIONS MAJOR, INDIANA UNIVERSITY

When my roommate's mom called me on her behalf to tell me that my roommate did not like my decorating ideas, I knew we were in for a long year!

ENGLISH AND THEATER MAJOR, DAVIDSON COLLEGE

*Never live with someone who could pass for Martha Stewart.*

GOVERNMENT/PSYCHOLOGY MAJOR, DARTMOUTH COLLEGE

**So it's now the second day of school.** All the parents have left and the dorm has quieted down. Even if you've talked with your roommate on the phone, things are different when you're alone, face to face. Where do you go from here? Try the following icebreakers:

☆ **Go book shopping with your new roommate.** Ask her about the classes she's taking and why she chose them. Commiserate on the required course you both have to take.

☆ **Explore the campus together.** Locate all the buildings so you are both not completely lost on the first day of classes. Check out the bulletin board at the Student Center. Plan to attend a concert or club meeting together.

☆ **Ask questions that lead to interaction**, such as "Can you help me get my computer hooked up to the Internet?"

☆ **Have dinner together in the dining hall.** Discuss the salad bar options or, better yet, scope out the hot freshmen!

# STUDENTS SAY: LIFE BEYOND YOUR ROOMMATE

It's happened plenty of times before. You're all set to hang out with your roommate . . . who has just fled the scene. Or you've decided to eat dinner together . . . and sat in total silence. Don't freak out. First of all, it takes time to become friends with some people. Second of all, it's perfectly okay if you wind up not being best friends. Listen to what students had to say on the subject:

No matter how close you are, having separate activities and occasionally doing things apart will broaden both of your social circles.

ENGLISH/THEATER MAJOR, DREW UNIVERSITY

My freshman roommate was in all the same classes as I was and was on the same sports team as I was. It was too much. We got on each other's nerves. ANIMAL SCIENCE MAJOR, TEXAS A&M UNIVERSITY

*It's fun to live with people you love, but in shared housing you need your own space and interests.*
HUMANITIES MAJOR, BOSTON COLLEGE

**C**olleges and universities are made up of students from different backgrounds, religions, races, and lifestyles. The first issue that every student must come to terms with is: NOT EVERYONE WILL BE LIKE YOU. Different doesn't mean wrong, bad, ignorant, or strange. It just means different. Be positive—having a roommate who is different from you isn't a problem. It's an opportunity to learn about her, yourself, and to make a new friend. Here are several steps to bring together roommates from different backgrounds:

➡ **Don't generalize.** Simple statements like "those people" or "they are all alike except you, of course" are inappropriate. We are all individuals.

➡ **Educate yourself.** The best way to avoid misunderstandings is to learn about your roommate. Ask questions about his background. Ask to see pictures of his family or go with him to his place of worship. Knowledge equals wisdom—and your roommate will respect your effort!

➡ **Establish respect.** She may not do things the way you would. She may believe in things that you don't. The key here is not to always agree, but to accept differences and celebrate the fact that each of us is entitled to our own beliefs and way of doing things.

Source: Herringshaw, Doris I., "Communicating Across Cultures" www.ohioline.osu.edu/flm01/FS03.html

## Unlikely Roommates

**Oscar and Felix from The Odd Couple**

Ernie and Bert from Sesame Street

**Jack, Chrissy, and Janet from Three's Company**

Gilligan and the Skipper from Gilligan's Island

**Snow White and the Seven Dwarves**

Shrek and Donkey from Shrek

Everyone you meet can add unique value to your life if the two of you are patient and persistent enough to figure each other out.

ENGLISH LITERATURE MAJOR, UNIVERSITY OF NOTRE DAME

# My freshman roommate was deeply conservative. She was eighteen and practically married to her boyfriend. I'm so the opposite of that, but I learned to respect her for being so confident in her beliefs.

ANTHROPOLOGY MAJOR, UNIVERSITY OF ARIZONA

*One of the most beautiful things about the roommate experience is that you are given the opportunity to coexist with a random person who has come to the same place you have along a totally different path than you traveled.*

PSYCHOLOGY MAJOR, UNIVERSITY OF ROCHESTER

One of my roommates was too nervous to tell me he was gay because he thought I'd move out. I guessed it anyway and finally worked up the courage to tell him that I knew. Strangely enough, it brought us closer together in a way because we weren't competing with each other for cute girls!

APPLIED PHYSICS MAJOR, COLUMBIA UNIVERSITY

You can't assume everyone hails from a diverse background. My roommate had never met a black person before and held a lot of stereotypical, stupid assumptions. It was hard to sit down and tell her that her racist views had to change if we expected to get along.

FINANCE MAJOR, GEORGETOWN UNIVERSITY

**Over time, I became more like him, and he more like me. What was different about each other at first ended up shaping our personalities.**

MATH MAJOR, COLUMBIA UNIVERSITY

I learned to keep an open mind and not be judgmental. Living with a roommate in college is a great experience, but the only way you can prosper from it is to abandon what you believe to be "normal."

COMMUNICATIONS/ADVERTISING MAJOR, STATE UNIVERSITY OF NEW YORK—BUFFALO

**Whether or not you're instant best friends with your roommate, you'll still be living in very close quarters for months to come.** The next chapter will take you through the day-to-day issues that might arise—and tell you how to deal with them.

# 3

# THE INS AND OUTS OF DAILY LIVING

*I grossly underestimated my roommate's ability to snore at a sleep-depriving decibel level.*

**ENGLISH MAJOR, RICKS COLLEGE**

# Learning how to share your space with another person is the biggest roommate lesson you will learn.

In a sense, you need to rewire your thinking so you can start considering someone else before you act (e.g., pumping up the volume of your music at 3:00 A.M. while your roommate is sound asleep before an early-morning exam is <u>not</u> going to make for an easy living situation).

The key is to THINK BEYOND YOURSELF. This chapter will help you do just that—plus offer advice on what to do if your roommate is the one who isn't being considerate of you!

**A**hhh, sleep. You've been hard at work all day, studying for your biology midterm. You shut off the lights, place your head on the cool pillowcase and close your eyes, slowly drifting into dreamland. Then—BLAM! The door bangs open and bright light fills the room. You hear your roommate click on his computer and the <u>tap, tap</u> of his keyboard. Good-bye restful sleep . . . hello, roommate confrontation.

Nothing is more precious to a college student than sleep. We all wish for more of it, and nothing makes us more cranky than someone messing with our shut-eye schedule. But unfortunately, very few roommates have the same class, exam, and social agenda. Here are some ways to steer clear of the problem:

1. **Find something to mask the noise.** A good option is one of those white noise machines. Drown out your roommate with the soothing sounds of a tropical rain forest or the rhythmic waves of the ocean. Another option is a pair of earplugs, which you can find in any drugstore. Pop 'em in and silence is yours.

2. **Find something to deflect the light.** Use an eye mask—when your roommate comes home late at night and flicks on the switch, you won't even realize a light is on.

3. **Keep movement to a minimum.** If you know you're going to be out late and will be coming home to a sleeping roomie, plan ahead. Clear the clutter off the floor before you go out so you can make it to your bed without tripping. Place your pj's on your bed for easier access. Take off your clunky heels or heavy boots *before* you enter your room so you're not clumping around.

4. **A little consideration please!** It's that good ole "do unto others" thing again. It is not a smart idea to wake your sleeping roomie to announce that you mixed beer and milk together and it didn't taste bad. Believe us, he's not going to care.

Note to roommate: It is NOT okay to hit snooze twenty times in a row starting at 6 A.M.!

JOURNALISM MAJOR, SYRACUSE UNIVERSITY

My roommate was on the swim team and had to be in bed at nine so he could wake up for practice at 4:30 A.M.! I joined a fraternity and was consequently often out late. We agreed that if I was quiet when I came back at night, he'd be quiet when he woke up in the morning.

INDUSTRIAL AND LABOR RELATIONS MAJOR, CORNELL UNIVERSITY

*When one of us wanted to go to bed early, we would turn off the ceiling light, but each of us had a small desk lamp that we would use while the other was sleeping.*

CRIMINAL JUSTICE MAJOR, STATE UNIVERSITY OF NEW YORK—ALBANY

If I was watching TV, I had earphones that I could plug into the bottom of the TV if my roommate wanted to sleep.

CRIMINAL JUSTICE MAJOR, GEORGE WASHINGTON UNIVERSITY

Use a fan with a towel over it to block out late-night noise when you want to sleep.

ENGLISH LITERATURE MAJOR, UNIVERSITY OF CALIFORNIA—LOS ANGELES

Definitely bring your own alarm clock. For a while, I shared an alarm clock with my roommate, and he always forgot to reset it. This caused me to miss a <u>lot</u> of classes!

AMERICAN STUDIES MAJOR, PROVIDENCE COLLEGE

My roommate and I had opposite going-to-bed/waking-up schedules. We solved this by buying a blue light bulb and putting it in our smallest lamp. This gave enough light to see by so someone didn't trip in the dark, but it wasn't bright enough to wake the person who was sleeping.

ART MAJOR, SKIDMORE COLLEGE

# LEAVE YOUR NAME, NUMBER, AND TIME YOU CALLED

**W**hether you are a hundred miles away from home or going to college in your hometown, the telephone provides the most intimate connection to the family and friends you've left behind. It also holds the promise of Saturday night plans with that special someone, possible information about changes in a study group locale, or a request for a summer job interview. For college students everywhere, the phone is near and dear to their hearts.

On the next few pages, college students discuss phone issues that come up between roommates and how they can be avoided. We wanted to mention the #1 phone offense up front: Taking messages. Don't be one of those roommates who:

★ **Trusts your memory.** When you take a message for your roommate, always write it down. There are too many plans for parties and multiple-choice test answers clogging up your brain to have any hope of remembering it.

★ **Leaves messages in hard-to-find places.** Your roommate won't find the message under yesterday's pile of dirty laundry. Leave the message somewhere where your roommate is sure to see it. It's a good idea to get a message board of some kind so messages can be seen as soon as someone enters the room.

★ **Decides which messages are not important.** Even if your roommate's ex-boyfriend has called ten times already, give your roommate every message. It is not for you to determine the merit of the message.

★ **Hears a different message than the one left.** If your roommate's friend calls and says she has to cancel their plans (again) for that night, your message should not read, "[friend's name here] apologizes for being a bad friend. She's canceling <u>again</u> but didn't mention how she was going to make it up to you." Stick to the facts.

★ **Feels the need to tell the caller where your roommate is, what she's doing, and her general life story.** Discuss beforehand how much information you and your roommate want you to give out to callers about whereabouts and time of return.

★ **Complains about feeling like your roommate's secretary.** Don't get angry and refuse to take messages—instead, talk to your roommate about it. There are lots of options, such as separate lines or distinctive rings.

## A WORD TO THE WISE:

If you are the one whom everyone is calling constantly, be proactive. First, tell your friends not to call repeatedly or let them know the best time to call. Second, go over this list with your roommate!

## STUDENTS SAY:
### WHEN THE MESSAGE ISN'T GETTING THROUGH

Even after I talked to her about it, my roommate always listened to my phone messages or "forgot" to give me messages. I finally told my friends to stop leaving messages and just call back until I answered.

**FILM STUDIES MAJOR, CARLTON COLLEGE**

**My roommate and I shared an answering machine, and we had problems doing that because messages would get erased. My solution was to go out and buy an answering machine with separate mailboxes.**

**POLITICAL SCIENCE MAJOR, GEORGIA SOUTHERN UNIVERSITY**

*I had a lot of friends and wanted to talk to them on the phone. She was always on the phone with her parents. We had to make a phone schedule.*

**FINANCE MAJOR, GEORGETOWN UNIVERSITY**

When I wasn't in the room, my roommate made long-distance calls on my phone. If I had not checked my phone bill, I would never have known. It was hard to confront him about this. He confessed and paid me back, but it was the fact that he tried to deceive me that forever bothered me.

**ENGLISH MAJOR, NORTH CAROLINA AGRICULTURAL AND TECHNICAL STATE UNIVERSITY**

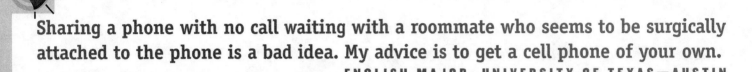

Sharing a phone with no call waiting with a roommate who seems to be surgically attached to the phone is a bad idea. My advice is to get a cell phone of your own.

ENGLISH MAJOR, UNIVERSITY OF TEXAS—AUSTIN

I had a lot of roommates, so we put a timer by the phone. We agreed to a time limit for conversations with friends on campus, since you can easily walk over and talk to them.

HISTORY MAJOR, COLLEGE OF CHARLESTON

*One of the smartest things we did was never have long-distance telephone service. That way we didn't have to divvy up a big bill. Everyone just relied on phone cards or calling collect.*

JOURNALISM MAJOR, UNIVERSITY OF IOWA

**Y**ou're back from class, but your roommate's still out. You open the mini fridge and spot a slice of chocolate cake. You know you didn't buy it, but it looks so good. You break off a piece—just for a taste. Then another piece. Soon, there are only crumbs left—oops!

You dash off for your next class. Five minutes later, your roommate comes back to the room. She has been dreaming of her chocolate cake all afternoon—she even bought a carton of milk to go with it. She opens the fridge and stares in horror at the crumbs. Let us tell you—small countries have gone to war for acts less egregious than this. You are in big trouble, my friend!

Sharing food without asking is a <u>very</u> sensitive topic. Students are highly proprietary over their Ramen Noodles, instant Mac 'n Cheese, ice cream, and whatever other small treats they can afford to cram into their fridge. To avoid an all-out food fight with your roommate, here are some tips to keep the grumbling inside your stomach:

- At the beginning of the school year, discuss what foods will be shared and what is off-limits. (Financially speaking, it's a good idea to share condiments and staples.)

- Give each roommate one shelf in the refrigerator for food that is solely his. Have one shelf for common food.

- Be courteous—never eat someone's last slice of bread or the leftover slice of pizza he's been saving.

- Do not let your friend or significant other eat the common food or your roommate's food. It's like a restaurant—if you don't pay, you don't eat.

- Don't blame missing food on Cookie Monster. If you ate it, own up.

- If you decide to share food, go shopping together and buy foods you both like. If one roommate goes out and purchases all the staples and condiments for the month, remember to reimburse your roommate for half (or whatever your agreed-upon share is).

- Try to keep it all in perspective. If your roommate ate a handful of potato chips, do not flip out. In the greater scheme of things, greasy slabs of starch are not important enough to fight over.

**Sharing food is like opening Pandora's box.** Once you give someone permission to have one thing, they will continue to take until you lay down the law.

PHYSICS MAJOR, UNIVERSITY OF CALIFORNIA—DAVIS

## Roommates do not have the gift of reading your mind. Telepathically screaming at her to stop using all the milk without replacing it won't solve the problem.

ENGLISH MAJOR, UNIVERSITY OF CALIFORNIA—SANTA BARBARA

*We wound up putting our initials on the food we did not want to share.*

JOURNALISM MAJOR, GEORGE WASHINGTON UNIVERSITY

If you're willing to always eat together, then you shouldn't have a problem sharing food with your roommate.

PSYCHOLOGY MAJOR, UNIVERSITY OF CALIFORNIA—SAN DIEGO

# PUMP UP THE VOLUME

**C**ontrary to popular belief, music does not sooth the savage in a college student. If anything, when your roommate and you have different tastes in music, the choice of tunes tends to aggravate the relationship. Here are some dos and don'ts that will help lead to a harmonious relationship:

## Do:

◎ Open your ears and take a moment to listen. You never know, you just may get into Gregorian chants.

◎ Find music that you both like (or can at least tolerate). If you can't find any in your collection, go shopping in the music aisle of the campus store together and pick up tunes for the room that you agree to play when you are both there. And save the music only you like for when you are alone in the room.

◎ Take turns playing your stereos or, if you share one, choosing the CDs.

## Don't:

◎ Criticize your roommate's music. Music preference is subjective—don't make it personal.

◎ Turn your dislike of your roommate's music into a battle of the bands, by pumping the volume of your music to drown out his. All you're going to end up with is a lot of loud noise.

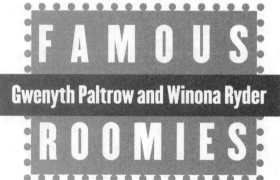

FAMOUS

Gwenyth Paltrow and Winona Ryder

ROOMIES

## STUDENTS SAY: THE BEAT GOES ON (AND ON)

We had different tastes in music, so we agreed to keep the music on at a low volume.

COMMUNICATIONS MAJOR, SHIPPENSBURG UNIVERSITY

I am a strictly R&B kind of person. My roommate is a country kind of girl. I tolerated her music and she learned to tolerate mine. I eventually came to like the Dixie Chicks!

PUBLIC JUSTICE MAJOR, OSWEGO STATE UNIVERSITY

*My roommate listened to her music too loudly. I kept turning it down and eventually she picked up on it.*

ACCOUNTING MAJOR, VALAPRAISO UNIVERSITY

My roommate brought the stereo. She was really into this sappy top forty tune, and she would put it on the stereo every night and keep repeating it until she fell asleep. It was torturous, but I put up with it because she let me use her stereo when she wasn't there.

ANTHROPOLOGY MAJOR, UNIVERSITY OF ARIZONA

# Invest in a good pair of cordless headphones!

WOMEN'S STUDIES MAJOR, SMITH COLLEGE

# STUDENTS SAY: STUDYING IN THE ROOM

Very few people have the same study habits. Since this is what you are paying big bucks to do, it is wise to establish the study rules up front. If your roommate can write a paper on Shakespeare while blasting heavy metal music, it doesn't mean you can. Figure out what works for both of you, like these students did:

My roommate and I decided early on that if one person had to stay up late and study and the other wanted to sleep, the person who wanted to study went to the study room downstairs in our dorm.

**BUSINESS ADMINISTRATION MAJOR, BOSTON UNIVERSITY**

**My roommate and I made a point of understanding each other's schedules, so that we knew not to have any guests over the night before one of us had a big test.**

**INTERNATIONAL STUDIES MAJOR, TEXAS A&M UNIVERSITY**

We had a rule never to use the other's desk to study from or eat on. No one wants to come back to his room to see the important papers on his desk shuffled around or to find crumbs.

POLITICAL SCIENCE MAJOR, STATE UNIVERSITY OF NEW YORK—ONEONTA

## We set an hour when it was time to stop studying in the room.

ENGLISH MAJOR, UNIVERSITY OF OREGON

*If one of us was studying in the room, the other was always respectful— no TV, no loud music, and no endless phone calls.*

ENGLISH/THEATER MAJOR, DREW UNIVERSITY

# STUDENTS SAY: PRIVACY

Roommates are privy to the most personal details of each other's lives. Together you will share your space and your secrets. If privacy is violated, rebuilding trust is very difficult. Look what happened to these students:

My roommate and I weren't getting along very well, and she wanted to know what I was thinking, so she read my journal! I was so angry that I didn't talk to her for a couple of days. She had the RA mediate, and we were able to talk out some of our issues.

BUSINESS ADMINISTRATION MAJOR, UNIVERSITY OF DELAWARE

*I caught my roommate reading my email.* *She apologized but said she thought it was okay because I didn't close the email on the computer when I left the room. I told her I didn't appreciate the disrespect of my privacy, but after that I always double-checked to make sure I shut off the email.*

COMMUNICATION MAJOR, SHIPPENSBURG UNIVERSITY

I knew my roommate was going through my desk when I wasn't there and taking my supplies. When I asked him about it, he denied it. Luckily I caught him in the act by leaving the room and coming back in when he wasn't expecting me—and then I talked to him about it.

PHILOSOPHY MAJOR, UNIVERSITY OF CALIFORNIA—DAVIS

I found my roommate going through my graded papers to compare how we were doing in the classes that we took together. I said that I'd prefer that he just ask me directly about my grades instead of going through my stuff.

POLITICAL SCIENCE MAJOR, UNIVERSITY OF MICHIGAN—ANN ARBOR

If your roommate has snooped in your email or you suspect her of doing it, it is easy to change the password on your email account.

◎ Do not make your password something that your roommate can easily figure out. Create a password containing a meaningless bunch of lowercase and uppercase letters, and numbers.

◎ Do not use the same password for all your Internet services and websites. People who find out one password can then use that same password to open your other accounts.

◎ Do not use the automatic log-in feature. Do not store your password in your computer, no matter how convenient it is.

You sit in a lecture hall with one hundred other students. You live in a dorm with two hundred other students. You share a room. Sometimes you feel so crowded that it's hard to hear yourself think.

College can be a stressful time, and it is important to have time for yourself—and the same goes for your roommate. Allow each other to have some space and spend time in the room alone. Remember, absence makes the heart grow fonder!

**It is important to always give each other plenty of space and private time, because you can only take so much of living that close with someone—no matter what good friends you are or how well you get along.**

**PSYCHOLOGY MAJOR, GEORGETOWN UNIVERSITY**

I wish I had made it clear to my roommate never to ask me a million questions about where I have been or what I did. If I wanted him to know everything, I would have told him.

MARKETING MAJOR, UNIVERSITY OF ALABAMA

*Personal time is a big concern. You have to be aware that each person needs the room to themselves every now and then*—and *it doesn't matter what the reason is.*

PRE-MED MAJOR, ST. MARY'S COLLEGE

**P**ersonal safety and the safety of your belongings is something all college students must consider. Would your parents invite strangers off the street to hang out in your bedroom? Definitely not. So why is your dorm room or apartment any different?

To ensure your safety, consider the following:

➤ **Assess the situation.** Talk to your roommate about what makes you feel safe in your room. Make sure all the entry-ways to your room or apartment close properly and are not accessible from the outside if you don't want them to be.

➤ **Lock the door.** It is a good idea to lock the door if you are the last person to leave the room—even if you'll be back shortly.

➤ **Entertaining strangers.** How do you feel about guests? What are your rules about letting people you don't know into your room or apartment? Discuss this all up front so you feel comfortable in your own home.

## STUDENTS SAY: SPACE INVADERS

One roommate gave her key to our apartment to her ex-boyfriend so he could live there over Christmas break, assuming we would never find out. But I came back early and was surprised to find him there. I waited a few hours to 'cool down' and then I called her to let her know I was very disappointed. You should never invade someone's space without consulting them first.

HISTORY/POLITICAL SCIENCE MAJOR, COLLEGE OF CHARLESTON

My freshman roommate would give out the key to our room to random freshmen. I came home around midnight one Saturday night to find two people "together" on my bed! I was very upset—I had assumed my roommate would realize that this was off-limits. I guess I shouldn't have assumed anything.

HISTORY MAJOR, BOSTON COLLEGE

*I was awakened in the middle of the night to find my roommate's friend standing in the middle of our room totally drunk and out of it. I sat up and yelled at him and made him leave. My roommate apologized for her friend's outrageous behavior and after that, we agreed to always lock our door at night.*

SOCIOLOGY MAJOR, NEW YORK UNIVERSITY

**My roommate didn't care about locking the door to our room. I thought we should always lock it, but after a while I just gave in and settled for always closing it, but not locking it. Looking back, we were very lucky that we were never robbed, and I shouldn't have let the issue drop.**

ETHICS MAJOR, YALE UNIVERSITY

# LIVE AND LET LIVE

**N**ow that we've covered the bigger issues, on the next few pages we'll leave you with the smaller ones to watch out for and one piece of advice: Be considerate when addressing a problem. Don't attack your roommate; instead, say that the problem is yours. ("I'm having a hard time sleeping with the TV on, and I have an early class tomorrow.") Then offer a solution. ("You can borrow my headphones," or "Tomorrow night I plan to be in the library late so you can watch TV then. How about taping the show?") When discussing the situation, remember to be reasonable. Reasonable goes a long way.

# STUDENTS SAY: IT'S A GAME OF GIVE AND TAKE

A surprising issue that often pops up is at what temperature to keep the thermostat. A room that is kept at a temperature that is far below or above what you are used to can make you miserable. Temperature is one of those things that you can and should compromise on.

FINANCE MAJOR, UNIVERSITY OF FLORIDA—GAINESVILLE

**I was a non-smoker; she was a smoker. We compromised by agreeing that she could smoke in our room only if she leaned out the window.**

PHILOSOPHY MAJOR, ANTIOCH COLLEGE

*My roommate liked to blow-dry her hair really early in the morning, while I was still trying to sleep. She agreed to do her hair in the bathroom instead.*

ART HISTORY MAJOR, WAKE FOREST UNIVERSITY

*My roommate and I set schedules for taking showers. Each person had priority at certain times.*

ENGLISH MAJOR, UNIVERSITY OF NORTH CAROLINA—CHAPEL HILL

My roommate liked to walk around our room naked. At first I was kind of weirded out by this, but as time passed, I got over it and got naked, too.

CRIMINAL JUSTICE MAJOR, GEORGE WASHINGTON UNIVERSITY

If there's one thing college students have pointed out in this chapter, it's that the foundation for being a good roommate is built upon **compromise.** Your motto should be: *This is OUR room. We both have a right to live here and both be happy.* If you stick with this frame of mind, compromise will come easily—just like it did for the students below.

Everything is a compromise, especially when you live in a dorm room. They are small and there really isn't enough space. You compromise on guests, quiet time, TV time, study time, lights-out time—all the time.

**JOURNALISM MAJOR, UNIVERSITY OF SOUTH CAROLINA**

Instead of compromising we harmonized our spaces, times, work/play habits. We got along and lived life without getting in each other's way.

**MATHEMATICS MAJOR, CORNELL UNIVERSITY**

**Be Zen in your interactions and don't let anything within reason bother you.**

SOCIOLOGY MAJOR, TULANE UNIVERSITY

**I lived with five other girls, so we often had "suite discussions" to compromise on whatever issues we felt were creating a hostile environment.**

SPANISH LITERATURE MAJOR, WASHINGTON UNIVERSITY—ST. LOUIS

Try to put yourself in your roommate's shoes before you react.

LAW MAJOR, GEORGETOWN UNIVERSITY

## Compromise—but don't be a doormat.

SPANISH MAJOR, UNIVERSITY OF KANSAS

*You have to be tolerant and adapt to your roommate. You do not come from the same place nor do you have the same background. It must be understood that both of you will have to make changes in order to have a good living experience.*

SOCIOLOGY MAJOR, YESHIVA UNIVERSITY

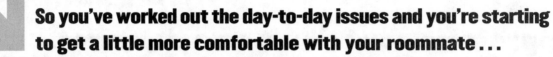

**So you've worked out the day-to-day issues and you're starting to get a little more comfortable with your roommate . . .**

until you realize there are no clean plates to eat your lunch on because they're all coated with food and piled on your roommate's desk. Instead of getting into an argument about this, read on to find out how to get some clean into your college scene.

# 4

## WE HAVE TO CLEAN IT OURSELVES?

*Don't let your roommate leave a bowl of cereal sitting underneath clothing for two months unless you really want to learn how yogurt is formed.*

**JOURNALISM MAJOR, SYRACUSE UNIVERSITY**

**The first thing college students learn when they move out of their parents' houses is,** surprisingly, if you don't clean something, it's actually NOT going to clean itself. And that means you and your roommate are going to have to take care of it. You're not going to have a problem if both of you are super-clean, or if you both prefer to live like slobs (hey, we're not here to stop you!). It's when you have a difference of opinion that the problems begin, and this chapter is full of advice from students on what to do about it!

**Y**our roommate is messy. Your roommate is dirty. Your roommate is slovenly. Your roommate is growing new life forms on his side of the room.

Some poor students wind up paired with the cleaning-impaired! Just like with many other roommate issues, it's best to deal with cleaning problems right away. Here's how to get out of the mess:

★ **Speak softly and carry a vacuum.** Start slowly and with humor. If your roommate's dirty laundry covers the room, ask him what color the floor is—it's been so long since you've seen it! Sometimes a gentle reminder is all it takes to kick-start someone into action.

★ **Pump up the volume.** If subtle hints aren't doing the trick, speak up. Come right out and say the knife permanently stuck to the floor with dried peanut butter bothers you. The trick is to blame the mess, not your roommate personally. Don't call her a "disgusting slob." Instead say you are having trouble breathing because her sheets haven't been changed in six months.

★ **Teach by example.** Don't clean in private; otherwise, your roommate may be tempted to believe you have a magical relationship with the cleaning fairy. Make sure your roommate is home when you scrub down your half of the room. Midway through your scrub-fest, turn to your roomie and ask if she wants to borrow your bottle of cleaning spray 'cause you're happy to share.

★ **Be prepared to compromise.** If you are an obsessive cleaner/organizer, realize that your behavior is your choice. Your roommate may be happy living amongst his clutter. Just ask that his mess stays on his side of the room.

★ **If the room gets unhygienic and your roommate won't lift a dust rag, it's time to visit your RA.** Sometimes a neutral third party can help convince your roommate to clear away the clutter.

# STUDENTS SAY: RANTS FROM THE REVOLTED

My roommate's favorite quote was "A clean room is a sign of a misspent life."

**ECONOMICS MAJOR, TUFTS UNIVERSITY**

**If cleanliness is next to Godliness, then my roommate and I lived on the fifth level of Dante's Inferno!**

**SOCIOLOGY MAJOR, TULANE UNIVERSITY**

*Halfway through the year, I found a pile of dirty, moldy dishes stashed under her bed!*

**ANTHROPOLOGY MAJOR, KENT STATE UNIVERSITY**

My freshman year roommate was my best friend from high school. It turned out that the reason his room at home was so clean was because of his mom—he had nothing to do with it. I didn't learn that until college.

**CRIMINOLOGY MAJOR, UNIVERSITY OF TAMPA**

It breeds resentment when you are ultimately responsible for all the cleaning.

ENGLISH MAJOR, GEORGETOWN UNIVERSITY

It's easy to become messy when your roommate is as well. Stop it before it starts!

INDUSTRIAL AND LABOR RELATIONS MAJOR, CORNELL UNIVERSITY

*I was a bit of a neat freak and she wasn't at all. We quickly learned to ignore each other's living spaces. We weren't there to be each other's moms—we were there to be friends.*

COMMUNICATIONS MAJOR, COLLEGE OF CHARLESTON

She kept leaving old food out. When I got sick of throwing it away for her all the time, I would leave it on her bed.

COMMUNICATIONS MAJOR, UNIVERSITY OF COLORADO—BOULDER

**We could not compromise on when the dishes should be done. I thought within a few days; she thought sometime next month. So I started putting her dirty dishes in her room—then she cleaned them.**

SOCIOLOGY MAJOR, NEW YORK UNIVERSITY

When one particular roommate was leaving her dirty dishes in the sink for days until others cleaned them, not-so-subtle Post-it® notes demanding she hit the sink and scrub would start appearing all over the apartment until she got the hint.

ENGLISH MAJOR, VILLANOVA UNIVERSITY

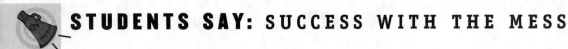

## STUDENTS SAY: SUCCESS WITH THE MESS

Sometimes you might have to remind your roommates that they need to mop the floor if you've done it three times and they never have. As long as you act like it's no big deal and you're asking—not telling—people will be okay with it.

PSYCHOLOGY MAJOR, UNIVERSITY OF CALIFORNIA—SAN DIEGO

Always show people the consequences of their actions. For example, if someone keeps leaving a mess in the kitchen, explain that it took you an hour to clean up and it cut into your study time. Or tell her you had to throw away your favorite plate because the cheese from her Hot Pockets® was left stuck on it for four days!

JOURNALISM MAJOR, OHIO UNIVERSITY

# STUDENTS SAY: THE MESS IS MINE

I don't think my roommate minded all my clutter, and I always made sure to tidy up before her mother came to visit, which was the only time she really seemed to care.

**GEOGRAPHY MAJOR, QUEEN'S UNIVERSITY**

**If my roommate's side of the room was clean and I didn't have the time or energy to clean my side, I hid my mess so she wouldn't have to look at it.**

**PHILOSOPHY AND LEGAL STUDIES MAJOR, HAMLINE UNIVERSITY**

*I feel bad because I never washed the dishes that my roommate brought. Halfway through the year we invested in disposable dishes and utensils, and then we got along so much better.*

**PSYCHOLOGY MAJOR, SAINT LEO UNIVERSITY**

# Your Mother is <u>Not</u> Here: Setting Up a Cleaning Schedule

When you live in an apartment or a house, the more space you have, the more space you have to clean. As anal as it might sound, a cleaning schedule is a very good idea. It stops the finger pointing. It doesn't allow for the assumption that someone else is going to do it. Scheduled cleaning results in more regular cleaning, especially since the schedule is usually ruled over by the person with the least tolerance for dirt.

Sit down with your roommate and decide who is going to do what. However you design it, make sure it is fair and equitable. Create a schedule when school first starts—the longer you put off this discussion, the thicker the mold will grow.

# STUDENTS SAY: SCHEDULE THE SCRUB

We had a cleaning wheel for the nitty-gritty stuff (i.e., scrubbing sinks, mopping floors, etc.). Each week we would rotate the wheel so the same person did not get stuck cleaning the toilet or taking out the trash.

**SPANISH LITERATURE MAJOR, WASHINGTON UNIVERSITY—ST. LOUIS**

**No one ever wanted to clean, so we decided to make a chore list and everyone had a different duty (e.g., cleaning the bathroom, vacuuming the living room) for the month that had to be completed at least once a week.**

**ANTHROPOLOGY MAJOR, KENT STATE UNIVERSITY**

*It is helpful to have a schedule of cleaning and chores before things get out of hand. You start the year off saying everyone will do his part and clean up after himself, but after a few weeks the place is a mess and everyone blames someone else.*

**GOVERNMENT MAJOR, CONNECTICUT COLLEGE**

We had a chore chart and that worked very well. Each week a different person was "'the enforcer," which meant that if someone was not doing her chore, it was up to the enforcer to tell that person to get on the ball.

POLITICAL SCIENCE MAJOR, VANDERBILT UNIVERSITY

Someone different cleans each week. There is a list of things to be done. That person has three days to accomplish them—Friday, Saturday, or Sunday. The person can spend however much time doing it, as long as it gets done.

COMPUTER SCIENCE MAJOR, UNIVERSITY OF ARIZONA

*At first, my roommate and I had a cleaning schedule, but she never stuck to it, and I always ended up doing all the work. Then I decided to do nothing and see if she would clean. After three weeks, I could no longer bear the mess so a friend of mine and I cleaned the whole apartment from top to bottom. My roommate came home and saw what we were doing, but she said nothing. However, from that day on she helped out more often, especially when I asked.*

HISTORY/ENGLISH MAJOR, McGILL UNIVERSITY

**Y**ou and your roommate make your beds every day. You both separate your white clothes from your red clothes when you do the wash. You've both even been known to use the vacuum cleaner. Obviously, you're not part of the horror stories found in this chapter. For those roommates who agree on staying relatively clean, here are some inexpensive ways to keep your dorm room spic-and-span:

1.  **Try baking soda.** For less than a dollar, you can mix it with a little water and clean the bathroom sink and shower and deodorize the refrigerator.

2.  **Get an electrostatic dust mop.** It's a quick way to avoid dust bunnies.

3.  **Stock up on antibacterial or disinfecting wipes.** They are great for cleaning the bathroom, easy-to-use, and stop the spread of the common cold.

4. **Buy a mini-vac.** Dragging the big, heavy vacuum from the closet down the hall and into your room takes effort, so more than likely, you'll leave the nacho crumbs on the desk or the dirt from your boots on the floor. If the vac is small, you can clean the mess as it happens.

5. **Go with your strengths.** Your roommate used to have a summer job at the Gap and can fold clothes like a pro. You find the hum of the vacuum soothing. Divide the work—let your roommate organize, while you tackle the dust. Everyone will be happier in the end.

What if neither of you is out to win the Mr. Clean award, but want to pitch in to keep the place looking respectable? Here are a few guidelines that have worked for students in the past:

None of us minded clutter, but I had a problem when clutter turned unhygienic. We cleaned when we got grossed out—that was the resolution of the issue.

ECONOMICS/SPANISH MAJOR, YALE UNIVERSITY

We had some basic rules . . . like make your bed every day.

POLITICAL SCIENCE MAJOR, RUTGERS UNIVERSITY

*The rule of thumb was to leave the room as though you would return with a guest.*

COMMUNICATIONS MAJOR, LEMAR UNIVERSITY

**We both agreed that during midterms and finals we would let the place get dirty, and we wouldn't yell at each other. We agreed to clean after our tests were finished.**

CRIMINOLOGY MAJOR, UNIVERSITY OF CALIFORNIA—IRVINE

You and your roommate have tried to clean, but it's just not your thing and your room or apartment is just as messy as always. In fact, it's gotten so your mess disgusts you. Short of renting a forklift, what should you do if all else fails? Here's a couple of ways to dig out of the dirt:

1. **Call in the professionals.**

   Hire a cleaning service or a maid for a once-a-month clean out. You usually can find some inexpensive services in the classifieds in the college paper. Split the bill.

2. **Barter.**

   The guy down the hall from you is compulsively clean. Offer to treat him to a large pizza if he straightens your room. You never know, he may say yes.

# GROOMING YOUR ROOMIE

**C**leanliness is not only about hospital corners on the bed and a floor so clean you could eat off it. Cleanliness extends to the person in your room as well. No one wants to live with someone who smells. In fact, bad hygiene is probably one of the biggest turnoffs, but it's not an easy subject to bring up, 'cause there's really no nice way to say it. Take a deep breath (actually, considering your roommate, maybe not so deep!) and get ready for a touchy conversation. Here are some guidelines to follow so that you don't hurt anyone's feelings:

- **The two-for-one deal.** Come back to your room from the store. Pull a can of foot deodorizer or a bottle of shampoo out of a bag. Tell your roommate the store was having a two-for-one special. Toss him one bottle—say it's a gift from you. Then back off and hope he enjoys his gift.

- **Hint, hint.** "Was your shower as cold as mine this morning?" "Do you like that new toothpaste with the mouthwash already in it?" Try the subtle approach first. Hopefully she'll get the hint.

- **When nothing works** . . . be open and tell your roommate (in private) that he must have been studying really hard, 'cause he sure needs a shower!

FAMOUS

Dustin Hoffman and Robert Duvall

ROOMIES

## STUDENTS SAY: WHAT'S THAT SMELL?

My roommate flatulated so often, we had to buy an air freshener.

PHILOSOPHY MAJOR, BRIGHAM YOUNG UNIVERSITY

My roommate's philosophy was "If you can throw the clothing against the wall and it doesn't stick, you can still wear it."

PRE-LAW MAJOR, PENSACOLA CHRISTIAN COLLEGE

*My roommate ate cans and cans of tuna fish in our room every day. She finally took the hint when, every time I walked into our room, I would mention how horrible it smelled.*

INTERNATIONAL BUSINESS AND MARKETING MAJOR, GEORGE WASHINGTON UNIVERSITY

My roommate's feet and her shoes always smelled, so I made her keep her shoes out of the room and we always kept a can of Lysol®.

LAW MAJOR, HAMLINE UNIVERSITY

My roommate wore the absolutely worst-smelling perfume. I finally told her I was allergic to it to get her to stop.

HISTORY MAJOR, UNIVERSITY OF TEXAS—AUSTIN

# Now that your dorm floor is shining and your room smells great, you decide to hang out at the student center and relax.

Your roommate's not home, but you spot a sweater of hers that you wouldn't mind wearing on the way over. It can't hurt to borrow it for a few hours, right? Not necessarily. The next chapter will delve into the world of sharing between roommates—what's okay to share, and what's off limits!

# 5

## WHAT'S MINE IS MINE AND
## WHAT'S YOURS IS MINE, TOO

*Never share clothes or boyfriends with your roommate—
both have the potential to wind up in the trash!*

**ANTHROPOLOGY MAJOR, KENT STATE UNIVERSITY**

**Think back. In preschool, if you were coloring with your most-favorite periwinkle crayon and the snot-nosed kid next to you wanted it, you'd be forced to share.**

If you shared, you'd be congratulated for playing nice. If you didn't, you'd be banished to time out. The rules were very clear-cut.

Fast-forward fifteen years. You and your roommate are sharing a space. Inside there are many items—several of them very important to you. Do you share nicely? Or do you hold on tight and yell: "Mine, mine—all mine!" With no teacher or parent to force you to share, what is the right way to act? In this chapter, students weigh in on what is fair to share and what is best kept to yourselves.

**M**ost people don't mind lending you a pencil or a tissue, but when it comes to bigger or more personal items, property rules should be established from the start. Many roommate problems start with miscommunication over sharing.

Here are some general rules to keep in mind when you choose to share:

◎ **If you have certain ways you want your property to be treated, let your roommate know.** If you don't want your CDs used as drink coasters, ask your roommate to please return them to their proper cases.

◎ **If you borrow something, always return it promptly in the same condition that you received it.** Get real— there is *no way* your roommate is going to believe the tire was flat on her bike before she lent to it you. Get it fixed. And, yes, she will miss it if you keep riding it to class every day this month!

◎ **Be honest about what you borrow from your roommate or if you lost or broke something.** If you break it, replace it. If you have absolutely no idea where you left his football after that awesome game in the snow, it's time to go shopping. That ball is *not* turning up after the first thaw!

- ◎ **Restock supplies.** If you used the last tissue, buy another box (even two) before your roommate gets a nasty cold and has to use your T-shirt to blow her nose.

- ◎ **Always ask first.** Just because you share the room does not automatically give you the right to share everything IN the room. Never assume that what is your roommate's is by proxy yours as well. Sure, all your towels are damp and dirty and your roommate's towels and clean, fluffy, and folded. That does not mean you are allowed to filch one.

# STUDENTS SAY: SHARING WORKS IF . . .

A sharing policy is good, but a "take-anything-when-you-need-it" policy can lead to unspoken resentment if one roommate feels taken advantage of.

ECONOMICS MAJOR, BRANDEIS UNIVERSITY

My roommate and I had an open relationship when it came to possessions. We were able to treat everything as "ours."

ENGLISH COMPOSITION MAJOR, DePAUW UNIVERSITY

*When sharing with your roommate, it really pays to be generous and easygoing.*

SOCIOLOGY MAJOR, TULANE UNIVERSITY

The secret to sharing successfully is to treat each other's belongings as if they were your own.

ENGLISH MAJOR, UNIVERSITY OF NORTH CAROLINA—CHAPEL HILL

Don't give your roommate the evil eye because she's drinking out of your Mickey Mouse cup while you are quite happily using her can opener.

PSYCHOLOGY MAJOR, UNIVERSITY OF CALIFORNIA—SAN DIEGO

A parking space—but we had to compromise on who parked there and when.

STATISTICS MAJOR, BOSTON COLLEGE

Food. It's a waste to have multiples of things like milk and butter.

ECONOMICS MAJOR, MICHIGAN STATE UNIVERSITY—EAST LANSING

*Clothes. Hello . . . two wardrobes instead of one!*

INTERNATIONAL COMMUNICATIONS MAJOR, TEXAS CHRISTIAN UNIVERSITY

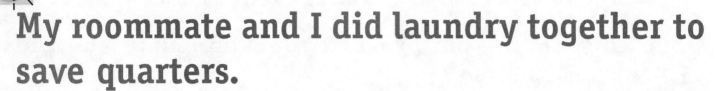

# My roommate and I did laundry together to save quarters.

POLITICAL SCIENCE MAJOR, TEXAS A&M UNIVERSITY—COLLEGE STATION

It helps to have one roommate buy the toilet paper and tissues one month, and the other roommate buys it the next month.

THEATER MAJOR, NEW YORK UNIVERSITY

# THE CLOTHING SWAP: PROCEED WITH CAUTION

**C**lothing is like a second skin. Nothing hugs your body closer than your favorite pair of jeans. Clothing is also infused with memories—like the skirt you wore when your boyfriend first said those three special words or the jersey you wore when you kicked the goal that won the game in overtime. So when your roommate borrows your skirt and it comes back with a chocolate stain or borrows your jersey and a hole mysteriously appear in the sleeve, emotions take over and conflict results.

Students report that, more often than not, sharing clothes leads to a war of the wardrobes. Here are some things to keep in mind:

➤ **Make it known from the start what clothes are off-limits and which ones are up for grabs.** Don't assume that if a never-been-worn sweater still has a tag on it, your roommate will know that she can't borrow it.

➤ **If your roommate lets you borrow something and you get a stain on it, wash it (and fold it!) before you return it.** Check the label first, though. If it says "dry-clean only," you'll need to shell out a few bucks and get it dry-cleaned.

- **If you ruin whatever clothing your roommate let you borrow, replace it immediately or offer to pay her for it.** It doesn't matter if it wasn't your fault—if you borrowed the clothing, you are responsible.

- **Return whatever you borrow.** Sure, your roommate said you can wear her fleece pullover whenever you want, but that does not mean it should reside in your closet.

- **Don't treat your roommate's closet like a store.** If you have no more white T-shirts, don't spend the rest of the year borrowing your roommate's. Go out and buy your own.

**FAMOUS ROOMIES**

Holly Hunter and Frances McDormand

Do not share your clothes with your roommate without a clear policy! You risk having your clothes mysteriously disappear—and you may see other people in your dorm wearing them as well.

ART HISTORY MAJOR, UNIVERSITY OF MARYLAND—COLLEGE PARK

I know it sounds like a good idea in the beginning to share clothes—especially for girls—but if something ever happens to your roommate's favorite sweater while you are wearing it, the tension in the room skyrockets!

ECONOMICS MAJOR, BUCKNELL UNIVERSITY

*If you borrow shoes and get them dirty, make sure you wipe them off before you give them back.*

COMMUNICATIONS MAJOR, COLLEGE OF CHARLESTON

You can only borrow your roommate's strapless bra for so long before you both need it on the same night. Get your own!

PSYCHOLOGY MAJOR, SAINT LEO UNIVERSITY

# SHARING NO-NO #1: THE COMPUTER

**W**hile there are many items that students share successfully, there are a few that students should never share.** When college students were asked which items they would <u>not</u> recommend sharing, the overwhelming #1 answer was the computer. Believe it or not, that box filled with electrical wires and microchips is a very personal, very private item. Think about this:

✮ **Your roommate suddenly drops out of school.** Off he goes—with your 40-page sociology thesis on his hard drive!

✮ **You're borrowing your roommate's computer.** You happen to take a look at her English term paper that's on her hard drive. Unconsciously, you use some of her ideas in your English term paper. Now you're being hauled into the dean's office for cheating!

✮ **Your roommate is forever online making new friends in every chat room imaginable.** It's not your computer, so you are forced to wait until 2 A.M., when she finally goes to sleep, to start your economics report.

* **Your roommate borrows your computer.** She's typing away and then—oops! She mistakenly deletes a whole semester's worth of your biology notes!

* **You log onto your roommate's computer.** You don't mean to, but your eye catches the subject line of one of his emails. One look at his private email won't hurt, right?

To make matters safe, byte the bullet and invest in your own computer or use the campus computer lab.

## A WORD TO THE WISE:

Many dorm rooms only offer one Internet connection, although there are two or more computers in the room. Hubs are a simple, compact way to connect two computers. Routers enable two computers to be online at the same time. Both can be purchased at stores that sell computer supplies.

## STUDENTS SAY: ONLY ONE MOUSE IN THE HOUSE

If one roommate has a computer and the other does not, there should be an agreement from the get-go about usage times or whether it will be shared at all.

**BIOLOGY MAJOR, SMITH COLLEGE**

## It's easy to think that sharing a roommate's computer will be fine, but usually deadlines for midterms and finals fall at the same point in the year for everybody.

**ETHICS MAJOR, YALE UNIVERSITY**

*Be careful sharing a printer. College students are poor and cartridges are expensive.*

**ENGLISH MAJOR, CASE WESTERN RESERVE UNIVERSITY**

Bathroom items—they are meant to be personal.

POLITICAL SCIENCE MAJOR, ALMA COLLEGE

A laundry bag—you don't want your dirty underwear mixed with your roommate's!

CRIMINAL JUSTICE MAJOR, GEORGE WASHINGTON UNIVERSITY

*Your car—for insurance purposes and because you don't know if your buddy will drive drunk.*

FINANCE MAJOR, UNIVERSITY OF FLORIDA—GAINESVILLE

**Your car—my roommate racked up quite a few parking tickets on mine.**

BUSINESS MANAGEMENT MAJOR, CALIFORNIA STATE UNIVERSITY

**Books, because you will need your own to use at any given moment.**

COMMUNICATIONS MAJOR, UNIVERSITY OF COLORADO—BOULDER

Anything that cannot be divided when you move out. Otherwise, you are left with the question of who keeps an item and if the other person should pay for it.

WOMEN'S STUDIES MAJOR, OKLAHOMA STATE UNIVERSITY—STILLWATER

Anything that requires cleaning after each use—like a George Foreman Grill—because chances are your roommate won't clean it well enough or at all.

ENGLISH MAJOR, UNIVERSITY OF TEXAS—AUSTIN

Anything you cannot afford to replace—just in case your roommate refuses to replace it.

GOVERNMENT MAJOR, CONNECTICUT COLLEGE

**T**here may be times when your roommate does not play by the rules, be it intentionally or inadvertently. If you catch your roommate using something of yours that was not on the "To Be Shared" list, here are two tips on what to do:

◘ **Communicate your displeasure in a friendly way.** Snapping at your roommate: "Why is my new white sweatshirt in your filthy closet?" doesn't help to resolve the problem. Instead try: "I just found my new white sweatshirt in your closet. Next time, I'd really appreciate it if you'd ask first."

◘ **Out of sight, out of mind.** If your roommate keeps taking your favorite CD even though you've asked him not to, avoid keeping it out in the open when you're not around. Yes, we're saying hide it!

# STUDENTS SAY: DON'T SHARE ANYTHING—EVER!

While many roommates get along just fine sharing each other's things, there are some students out there who believe that sharing will lead to problems, period. Here's what they had to say:

In any other environment, sharing a box of tissues or a bag of chips is no big deal. But in college, when people are mega-stressed, any little thing can seem like a big deal—especially when someone finishes off the entire big bag of chips or uses the last tissue.

APPLIED PHYSICS MAJOR, COLUMBIA UNIVERSITY

**In all my college years, despite being close friends with my roommate, we never pooled resources. Perhaps that is why we remained closed friends.**

ENGLISH AND THEATER MAJOR, DREW UNIVERSITY

*We shared nothing. We literally drew a line down the middle of the room. Really, we did.*

ENVIRONMENTAL SCIENCE MAJOR, EMORY UNIVERSITY

## STUDENTS SAY: SHARING GOSSIP

As big as your dorm may seem, it is actually a very insular world and word travels fast. Gossip about your roommate is sure to come back to haunt you. If your roommate didn't pay for his half of the pizza or cheated on her boyfriend with the guy down the hall, don't tell anyone in your building. As juicy as gossip is, it can be a double-edged sword—your roommate probably knows just as much about you as you do about her. A good idea is to agree to live by the motto: *Whatever happens in our room, stays in our room.*

**Don't gossip about your roommate. It only reflects poorly on you.**

FRENCH MAJOR, EMORY UNIVERSITY

**When you live with other people, they know all your business. The worst is when they decide that since they know, they might as well tell others. That really breaks trust.**

BUSINESS MAJOR, WASHINGTON COLLEGE

One time I found out that my roommate had said something about me behind my back. It was something that I had told her in confidence. I talked to her about it and let her know it hurt my feelings. Nothing like that ever happened again. **INTEGRATED MARKETING MAJOR, EMERSON COLLEGE**

**You're starting to settle into your routine. You and your roommate have worked out everyday situations and it appears to be smooth sailing ahead.**

Then, a significant [or not-so-significant] other enters the picture. Great. Now you have a whole new set of problems to deal with! The next chapter will help you deal gracefully with any, ahem, uncomfortable situation you might come across.

# 6

# THE SIGNIFICANT OTHER

*Never assume your roommate is asleep!*

LEGAL STUDIES MAJOR, UNIVERSITY OF MASSACHUSETTS—AMHERST

**You and the hottie from down the hall are entwined in a down-and-dirty lip lock. Suddenly the door bangs open and in barges your roommate.**

As he clicks on the computer to check IMs, the steam from your kisses turns cold. Welcome to dorm room luvin'!

   With two or more people sharing a small space in a hormonally charged dorm, romance is sure to fire up problems unless rules and boundaries are set right away. In this chapter, college students weigh in on the rules of hooking up, what to do when both roommates need the room for love, and how to signal to your roommate that the room is otherwise "occupied" without being rude.

**M**aybe your boyfriend wants to spend every minute with you. Maybe you want to be with your girlfriend all the time. Sounds like the perfect plan—if you lived alone! Students warn that having your boyfriend or girlfriend in your room 24/7 is bound to create major roommate tension. The living space is small, and even if your roommate gets along really well with your significant other, hanging out with the two of you day in and day out is not what she signed on for. Here are some tips to keep you and your roommate happy:

⭐ **Don't step over the line.** Make sure your significant other knows the boundaries. He may be close with you, but this is not his room. The fridge is not a free-for-all. It is not okay for him to lounge on your roommate's bed.

⭐ **Be proactive.** If your significant other is becoming a nuisance to your roommate, <u>you</u> are the one who needs to talk to your romantic interest—not your roommate.

⭐ **Alternate.** Share the love and don't overextend your roommate's hospitality. Alternate between your significant other's place and yours.

⭐ **Keep PDAs to a minimum.** Do you want to witness your roommate's girlfriend groping him? Not a chance! Well, it goes the same way for your roommate, too. Keep your hands to yourselves when the two of you are not alone.

FAMOUS
Lindsay Lohan and Raven Simone
ROOMIES

A significant other could spend the night if we asked first, and the other roommate would spend the night at a friend's. But we agreed that at exam or finals time visitors were not allowed.

BIOCHEMISTRY/ MOLECULAR BIOLOGY MAJOR, BOSTON COLLEGE

We would try to disappear as much as possible to leave the other one alone if one of our boyfriends was over.

INTERNATIONAL RELATIONS MAJOR, SAN FRANCISCO STATE UNIVERSITY

*If my boyfriend and I wanted some alone time and my roommate was around, we'd always leave the room and find someplace else on campus to go. Who wants to be in a loud, unromantic dorm room with your love interest anyway?*

PUBLIC RELATIONS MAJOR, UNIVERSITY OF GEORGIA

# THE THIRD ROOMMATE

**W**hat happens if you're the one who's flying solo for the moment, but your roommate has a boyfriend or girlfriend who's always around? Here are some ideas for peace, love, and understanding:

✮ **Play nice.** Your roommate likes this guy so we're sure she'd appreciate it if you try to be nice to him (even if you can't for the life of you figure out why she'd want to date such a loser).

✮ **Have a private conversation.** If your roommate's girlfriend is annoying you to no end or has turned your desk into her own private vanity, confront your roommate, but do it without his girlfriend present. (Make an appointment with him to talk alone if you have to.) Try to have a clear and rational conversation. Do not criticize his girlfriend or accuse him of being "whipped"—instead offer some solutions to the problem.

✮ **Knock first.** If you think there's a good chance your roommate's significant other is there, knock before barging in. True, you have a right to enter your own room, but you should also respect your roommate's privacy. (Plus it might save you from seeing something you just don't want to see!)

* **Discourage PDAs.** If your roommate's displays of affection are more than you are comfortable witnessing up close and personal, tell her. It is okay to make rules like "No hooking up in the room if the other roommate is there." Remember it is your home, too, and you get an equal say as to what can or cannot happen.

* **Avoid the third-wheel syndrome.** Your roommate used to go to the dining hall every night with you for dinner and now he brings his girlfriend, too. Your roommate used to listen to the daily saga of your crush on that hot senior, but now her boyfriend is always adding his (unhelpful) opinions. Don't let yourself be dragged down because your roommate has hooked up. Search out the unattached in your dorm—they're sure to be a lot more fun than your roommate is these days!

**FAMOUS ROOMIES**

**Gene Hackman and Al Pacino**

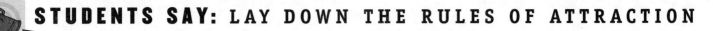

## STUDENTS SAY: LAY DOWN THE RULES OF ATTRACTION

I would often wake up in the middle of the night to hear my roommate and her boyfriend making out above me in the top bunk when they thought I was asleep. **NOT OK!** To avoid having to crawl out of your room commando style because you are too embarrassed to say something at that moment, talk about what to do ahead of time—<u>before</u> it becomes an issue.

LEGAL STUDIES MAJOR, UNIVERSITY OF MASSACHUSETTS—AMHERST

## When my roommate wanted to take "naps" with his girlfriend, I would take an elongated shower and a leisurely shave.

PROGRAM II MAJOR, DUKE UNIVERSITY

When my roommate's boyfriend visited, I left the room and I always gave her an approximate time of when I would return.

HISTORY MAJOR, COLORADO UNIVERSITY—BOULDER

My freshman year roommate's boyfriend was forever coming over to make out with her after I fell asleep. The trouble is, that with just a few feet between beds, even the heaviest sleeper is going to wake up with that kind of thing going on. My roommate would die if I ever told her what I saw!

HISTORY MAJOR, DUKE UNIVERSITY

I wish I had told my roommate that I minded when her boyfriend slept over instead of trying to avoid a fight. As a result, I think he spent more time in my room than I did!

BUSINESS ADMINISTRATION MAJOR, UNIVERSITY OF DELAWARE

# THE "BOOTY CALL" COMMANDMENTS

**H**ave you ever been in the situation where you come home to repeatedly find your roommate rolling around with some guy or girl that you've never seen before? There are special roommate rules for this kind of casual situation. Whether it's you or your roommate who's doing the hooking up, be mindful of the following commandments:

1.  **Thou shalt not** take your roommate's condoms and leave him stuck for Saturday night.

2.  **Thou shalt not** leave any evidence of a romantic encounter.

3.  **Thou shalt not** get hot and heavy with someone five minutes before your roommate is due home.

4.  **Thou shalt not** have an all-night Barry White love-fest while your roommate is cooling her heels in the lounge.

5.  **Thou shalt not** have relations on your roommate's bed, desk, towels, or side of the room.

6.  **Thou shalt not** hook up while your roommate is in the room—awake or asleep.

We would tell the other to leave the room. This was one of the advantages of being roommates with someone who is your friend.

NUTRITION MAJOR, STATE UNIVERSITY OF NEW YORK—STONY BROOK

With random hook ups, both roommates often feel that their privacy is compromised. The one hooking up feels he or she deserves a little privacy to boogie down in the room, and the other roommate feels he or she deserves to be able to enter his or her own room when he or she wants to. You've got to talk this out, so there's equal give-and-take from both of you.

GOVERNMENT MAJOR, GEORGETOWN UNIVERSITY

We promised to never "sexile" each other (kick your roommate out of the room for the purposes of hooking up). If that meant waiting until the other one was out of the room, then so be it!

POLITICAL SCIENCE MAJOR, NEW YORK UNIVERSITY

# STUDENTS SAY: FLIP YOU FOR IT

Sometimes you both get lucky at the same time on the same night (hey, we can all hope, right?), but there's only one room. You don't need to be a math major to see that this has the makings of a problem. Here's what students advise:

**If you have a common room, it is good to have a pullout couch, because it comes in handy if you share a bedroom.**

CRIMINAL JUSTICE MAJOR, GEORGE WASHINGTON UNIVERSITY

**Don't forget that the person you are hooking up with has a place to live, too. You need to compromise and have one roommate go elsewhere.**

ANTHROPOLOGY MAJOR, UNIVERSITY OF WESTERN ONTARIO

*If my roommate and I both needed the room, we would rock-paper-scissors for it.*

PRE-MED MAJOR, ST. MARY'S COLLEGE

# STUDENTS SAY: THE SIGNS OF LOVE

The most well-known and time-honored signal that the room is "occupied" is the good 'ole sock around the doorknob. However, if you are more electronically inclined, beepers, cell phones, and text messages also do the trick and leave little room for misunderstanding between roommates.

Here are some other highly effective ways to send your roommate a signal:

We placed a code word on the dry-erase board hanging outside our door. BONZAI!!! was the signal to find someplace else to sleep.

POLITICAL SCIENCE MAJOR, PENNSYLVANIA STATE UNIVERSITY

We developed a system where the privacy-seeking roommate would lock the door and put a piece of clear tape over the lock, so if the other roommate came home to discover the door locked and taped, she would know not to come a-knockin'.

ECONOMICS MAJOR, BUCKNELL UNIVERSITY

We placed a hairband on the handle outside if we wanted to be alone.
POLITICAL SCIENCE MAJOR, SHIPPENSBURG UNIVERSITY

**"We need milk" was the code word for the dry-erase board.**
FOOD SCIENCE MAJOR, ALMA COLLEGE

We had a knock pattern.
FINANCE/COMMUNICATION MAJOR, UNIVERSITY OF SOUTH FLORIDA

# We would put a tie on the door.

ECONOMICS MAJOR, VANDERBILT UNIVERSITY

**We would leave a sleeping bag outside the door—obviously that meant someone was going to be sleeping on the couch downstairs!**

SPANISH/HISTORY MAJOR, WILLAMETTE UNIVERSITY

*We worked out a signal on the door: we had a little paper heart laminated and we would stick it on the door if we brought someone back with us. The other person would then knock twice and say she'd be back in a few minutes.*

PSYCHOLOGY MAJOR, UNIVERSITY OF ILLINOIS—URBANA-CHAMPAIGN

# BREAKING UP IS HARD TO DO

**Y**ou come home from class and your roommate is trying to punch through the cinder-block wall or is in tears, rocking back and forth in the fetal position. You don't have to be a detective to know that your roomie was dumped. Now you are left to pick up the pieces of your roommate's pulverized heart. Here are some tips to help the healing process:

1. **Listen.** Even if that means enduring the eighty-fifth retelling of the story of how they were meant to be together and hearing the same sappy CD of "their song" over and over.

2. **Sympathize.** A broken heart hurts immensely. This is not the time for "I told you so's."

3. **Go fishing.** Okay, not literally. But when the wallowing in grief has run its course, motivate your roommate to forget about his sorrows. Show him that there are "plenty of fish in the sea" and head with him to a party, a bar, or a club meeting.

4. **Bite your tongue.** It's fun for your roommate to trash her ex—and it does make her feel better!—but before you join in the bashing, think about this: There's a very good chance that your roommate and the guy she hates today will kiss and make up tomorrow . . . and that she'll always remember you bad-mouthing her sweetie.

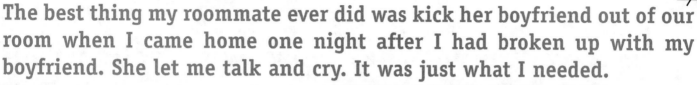

# STUDENTS SAY: HOW TO SURVIVE THE BREAKUP

The best thing my roommate ever did was kick her boyfriend out of our room when I came home one night after I had broken up with my boyfriend. She let me talk and cry. It was just what I needed.

POLITICAL SCIENCE MAJOR, BARNARD COLLEGE

One of my roommates went through a period of depression and self-destructive behavior after she broke up with her long-term boyfriend. All the other roommates agreed to never let her be by herself. We tried to keep her entertained to keep her mind off things.

ENGLISH MAJOR, UNIVERSITY OF CALIFORNIA—SANTA BARBARA

*Always agree that [the ex] was clearly out of his or her mind.*

JOURNALISM MAJOR, UNIVERSITY OF SOUTH CAROLINA

Even if you're not that close with your room-mate, **for girls, hugs are key.**

INTERNATIONAL AFFAIRS MAJOR, GEORGE WASHINGTON UNIVERSITY

For girls, Ben & Jerry's cures all!

PSYCHOLOGY MAJOR, GEORGETOWN UNIVERSITY

*If your roommate is a guy, just get him drunk and laid.*

HISTORY MAJOR, COLUMBIA UNIVERSITY

And while most roommates do not recommend sharing significant others, sometimes the unconventional route is the one that pays off. . . .

# I passed a guy off to my roommate, and she ended up marrying him!

SOCIOLOGY MAJOR, PENNSYLVANIA STATE UNIVERSITY

**Hooking up puts the excitement in college life, but college students would be nowhere without their friends.**

Turn the page to find out how to deal with keeping the social scene and your roommate situation in a perfect balance.

# 7

# SOCIAL HOUR

*My roommate and I agreed that neither of us would throw parties in our apartment. Our philosophy is: We should never trash our own home when we can just as easily trash someone else's!*

**URBAN PLANNING MAJOR, UNIVERSITY OF CINCINNATI**

**Dealing with the social scene at college is hard enough, but when you have a difference of opinion with your roommate on the matter,** dealing with it in your living space can be much more difficult. If you and your roommate share all the same friends, chances are there won't be a problem. But what if one of you is a party animal and one isn't? Or you have totally different friends . . . who can't get along? This chapter will tell you how to have a good time while keeping the peace on the home front.

# WHEN YOU CAN'T STAND YOUR ROOMMATE'S FRIENDS

**Y**ou've tried, we know you have, but you just can't deal with your roommate's friends. Every time you open your door, there they are . . . sitting on your bed, commenting on your life, or, even worse, outright ignoring you. If you don't like your roommate's friends, here are some suggestions for what to do:

- **Don't criticize them.** This will only make your roommate defensive and angry with you. Instead, mention in concrete terms why you find it hard to study with them always around or why you'd prefer they not riffle through your CD collection.

- **Be as friendly as possible.** If you get to know them a little, there might be qualities about them that you actually like, which will make them easier to deal with. For example, you both may love Rocky Road ice cream or cover your ears every time that girl from down the hall sings in the shower.

- **Tactfully attempt to motivate them to go elsewhere.** Suggest activities that may interest them to leave the room. "Hey, I heard they're giving away free pizza in the dining hall. . . ."

## STUDENTS SAY: NO FRIEND OF MINE

I really didn't like my roommate's friends. I told her that I didn't want them around when I was in the room. After that, her friends never hung out in our room, but my roommate and I never had a good relationship either. I should have handled the situation in a more sensitive manner.

INFORMATION TECHNOLOGY MAJOR, RENSSELAER POLYTECHNIC INSTITUTE

Whenever I came home from class, my roommate was there with her "clan." I felt like my privacy was being violated, but I didn't talk to her about it, because I didn't want to rock the boat. Instead, I said nothing and avoided being in my own room, which only made me resent her. I should have said something instead of keeping it all inside.

HISTORY/ENGLISH MAJOR, McGILL UNIVERSITY

**My roommate's friends were always around. The best choice I made for my social well-being was joining a sports team and becoming involved in groups on campus. I was so busy that I didn't care about all the people in my room.**

POLITICAL SCIENCE MAJOR, BOSTON COLLEGE

One of my roommates constantly brought a group of people over—never asking the others if it was an appropriate time. Our walls were really thin and we could hear everything. Eventually my other roommates and I had to talk to her about this, and she agreed to spend equal time at her friends' places.

PSYCHOLOGY MAJOR, UNIVERSITY OF ALABAMA

# CAN I GO, TOO?

**Y**ou and your friends decide to make a midnight run for spicy chicken wings and your roommate asks to come. You and your friends decide to play Frisbee on the quad and your roommate wants to join in. You and your friends decide to get flu shots and your roommate wants in too! What's a person to do when your roommate is always butting in on your plans? Before you go all *Single White Female,* read on for tips to gracefully avoid the "hanger-on syndrome."

➤ **Try to understand where your roommate is coming from.** Maybe she's never had to act independently before because she's always shared a room with a sibling or had a best friend by her side. Don't make fun of your roommate to your friends or try repeatedly to ditch her when she wants to come along. The passive-aggressive approach won't work and will only hurt your roommate's feelings.

➤ **Set limits.** Make specific plans for the two of you (Monday night at the dining hall or Thursday night for pizza) and then be clear that you have made other plans that don't include your roommate on the other nights.

➤ **Be straight with your roommate.** If all else fails, very nicely tell your roommate that she has been a bit intense lately and that you think you'd stay better friends if you each gave the other some space now and then.

# STUDENTS SAY: BEWARE OF THE LIFE-SUCKERS

My roommate was younger than I was, and she was very clingy as she tried to adjust to her new lifestyle. She made me feel smothered. I tried to get her to do things—without me—by telling her about events around campus that she was interested in, but knew I wasn't!

**SOCIOLOGY MAJOR, MESSIAH COLLEGE**

My freshman roommate was always trying to hang out with me and my friends. She was also scared to sleep in her own bed unless her boyfriend was over. If he wasn't there, she'd crawl into bed with me in the middle of the night! To solve it, I had to talk to her and tell her I liked her, but I needed to have alone time with my friends, and I definitely needed my bed to myself!

**POLITICAL SCIENCE MAJOR, UNIVERSITY OF HOUSTON**

My roommate was very clingy. Another one of my friends needed attention all the time. I thought that she would love to have someone who would follow her around and listen to everything she had to say. So I introduced her to my roommate—and just as I predicted—they clicked and became instant friends and my roommate was able to give me more space.

**JUSTICE STUDIES MAJOR, ARIZONA STATE UNIVERSITY**

# STUDENTS SAY: WHEN FRIENDS COME TO STAY

Sometimes your roommate's friends drop by your room to say hi . . . and never leave. Sometimes your roommate will invite a friend from home to stay over . . . for two weeks. To avoid any conflict that could result from this kind of situation, it is important for you and your roommate to answer the following questions up front: Where will guests sleep? How long may a guest stay? How will you communicate to each other when visiting hours are over? Here are some student suggestions:

I liked my roommate's friend until she started sleeping in our dorm room more often than not. She would eat our food, be in the way, and annoy me when I was studying. I fixed the situation by asking her to contribute to our food fund and be listed on our weekly cleaning tasks. These requests made her realize how much time she was spending in our room—she started coming around a lot less often.

JUSTICE STUDIES MAJOR, ARIZONA STATE UNIVERSITY

*If you have a friend visiting, don't take advantage of your roommate's hospitality. Remember it is his room just as much as it is yours.*

COMPUTER SCIENCE MAJOR, NEW YORK UNIVERSITY

There are many cases where one roommate has no problem with "social drug use" and the other roommate does. If your roommate is doing something illegal or something you are morally opposed to in your shared living space, students advise to stand your ground. You should never be made to feel uncomfortable in your own home. Speak up!

My roommates would always smoke pot in our room. I'd ask them to stop but they wouldn't. I complained that I was severely allergic to smoke (not true). After that, they tried to smoke outside the room.

CHEMICAL ENGINEERING MAJOR, COOPER UNION

The most difficult conversation I ever had with my roommate was when I told her that she couldn't keep using illegal drugs in our house. She got really angry at me and acted like I was messing up her life—but she did take her drugs elsewhere.

CRIMINAL JUSTICE MAJOR, UNIVERSITY OF NEVADA—LAS VEGAS

*It was really hard to work out an agreement with my roommate to keep illegal drug use out of the common room in our house. He kept "forgetting" about it and I kept reminding him. It took a while, but it finally worked.*

ENGLISH LITERATURE MAJOR, UNIVERSITY OF NOTRE DAME

**One of my roommates was a serious drug user. To get her to stop, we had to threaten her with eviction.**

ELECTRICAL ENGINEEERING MAJOR, TEXAS A&M UNIVERSITY

**When it comes to drugs, dropping subtle hints does not work—it really only pisses people off. You need to confront them head-on.**

TELECOMMUNICATIONS MAJOR, INDIANA UNIVERSITY

# IF YOU MAKE A PASS, YOU'D BETTER HAVE A FOOTBALL

You want to be close to your roommate, which to most of us means hanging out, gossiping, maybe catching a movie together. But sometimes, much to your surprise, your roommate will have sexual feelings toward you and want to get much closer—when you don't. Here's how to handle the situation, should it happen to you:

My roommate tried to kiss me. I just backed away and we never spoke of it afterward. Our friendship went stale. We should have talked about it—maybe things would be okay now.
**PSYCHOLOGY MAJOR, UNIVERSITY OF CALIFORNIA—BERKELEY**

My sophomore year roommate was bisexual, and I knew that he was attracted to me. It could have been a really uncomfortable situation, so I told him that I was flattered if he really was attracted, but I wasn't interested. He took it well, and he joked about it when he felt he needed to look away when I changed clothes. He was a great roommate.
**PSYCHOLOGY MAJOR, COLLEGE OF WOOSTER**

My roommate told me he wanted to date me. I didn't feel the same way so I told him that I was extremely flattered but I hoped I hadn't given him the wrong impression—I make it a point to never ever get involved in any type of romantic relationship with someone I live with.

PHYSICAL THERAPY MAJOR, TULANE UNIVERSITY

The key is to handle the situation with sensitivity. Try not to bruise egos or embarrass the other person.

BIOLOGICAL SCIENCES MAJOR, CORNELL UNIVERSITY

*You can always try setting him up with a friend!*

ENGINEERING MAJOR, DARTMOUTH COLLEGE

**C**ongratulations! You and your roommate are actually getting along and want to throw a social event together. Here are a few pointers to make sure that the party runs smoothly—and that there are no hard feelings when it's all over. Decide together:

◎ **A date that works for both of you.** Be understanding—if your roommate has a midterm the next day or a huge paper to write, no party.

◎ **Who will be invited.** Do you really need to invite your acquaintance from Chem 207 when you know your roommate can't stand him? Think about the greater good.

◎ **How big the party will be.** In some cases, size does matter.

◎ **The confines of the party.** Discuss if any rooms or items will be off-limits during the party. Respect your roommate's requests.

◎ **Money matters.** Agree on how much you each want to chip in for alcohol or soda and make sure there are no hard feelings afterward.

◎ **The morning after.** Agree to clean up together—no matter if you're hung over, if you've hooked up, or if the smell of half-eaten pizza disgusts you.

My roommate was an Internet junkie. She would meet all these weird people on the Internet and then would invite them to our place for parties. I finally had to tell her that she couldn't have a bunch of strangers in our house while I was there—it was just too creepy for me.

ENGLISH MAJOR, UNIVERSITY OF TORONTO

I once threw a huge party without letting my roommates know. They came home expecting to study and found three-foot speakers in the windows, a disco ball hanging from the ceiling, and about one hundred people in our house. They were not too happy—I guess I should have mentioned it first!

PSYCHOLOGY MAJOR, GEORGETOWN UNIVERSITY

My roommates and I learned the hard way that it is best to confine parties to common areas in a living space. Nothing ruins a good time better than someone spilling a drink on your bed or on your roommate's computer.

ENGLISH MAJOR, SIENA COLLEGE

Because the same people always seemed to be cleaning up after our parties, we made a list of our names and posted it on the wall. For every party, there were two of us assigned to clean and then our names would get crossed off. This way everyone had a turn.

SPANISH MAJOR, ROGER WILLIAMS UNIVERSITY

*Parties that try to incorporate all the roommates are the most fun and the most successful. That way everyone is invested in the process.*

MUSIC MAJOR, UNIVERSITY OF CALIFORNIA—SAN DIEGO

## So you think you've mastered the dorm and you're ready for the big leagues—living off-campus.

But moving out to your own house or apartment brings new roommate issues to your doorstep. The next chapter will tell you what they are—and how to deal with them!

# 8

# THE UPS AND DOWNS OF LIVING OFF-CAMPUS

*My roommate wouldn't pay the rent so I had to take her to court.*
*Can you believe she countersued me for emotional distress?*

**FILM STUDIES MAJOR, CARLETON COLLEGE**

**Thinking of living off-campus? Sounds good—more freedom, more independence, more space, more privacy.** No more bathrooms shared by thirty people, no more noise when you want quiet time to study. What could be better?

Keep in mind that living off-campus means more bills, responsibilities, and liabilities. In this chapter, students weigh in on everything from signing a lease to buying furniture.

**Y**ou've spent one year, maybe even two or three, in the dorms on campus and now you think you're ready to set out for the great beyond—an apartment off campus that you don't have to go through the university housing office to get. Before you make the leap, think about the pros and cons. On one hand there's more freedom to invite your entire basket weaving class over to complete a class project; on the other hand, there are more rooms to clean and cabinets to stock, as well as more financial responsibilities (Whose turn is it to buy toilet paper <u>this</u> week?). Hmmm, to go or not to go? On the next few pages students weigh in on what they think are the pros and cons to the situation.

# STUDENTS SAY:
## ROOMMATE PROS TO LIVING OFF-CAMPUS

When you live off-campus you have more space, which is a big plus. It makes things easier with roommates if you have a place to escape to.

CHEMICAL ENGINEERING MAJOR, COOPER UNION

When you live off-campus you don't have to live on top of another person's mess. Your roommate's mess can stay behind the closed door of her own room.

JOURNALISM/POLITICS MAJOR, NEW YORK UNIVERSITY

*Living off-campus you finally get a sense of real independence. No more RA to solve your problems. It's just you and your roommates—and you figure it out together.*

ELECTRICAL ENGINEERING MAJOR, UNIVERSITY OF LOUISVILLE

**Most dorms have a cleaning service for the bathrooms. In an apartment, there are often issues with cleaning the bathroom and kitchen.**
INDUSTRIAL AND LABOR RELATIONS MAJOR, CORNELL UNIVERSITY

If you have cars, taking turns with the only available parking space.
BIOLOGY MAJOR, UNIVERSITY OF CALIFORNIA—IRVINE

When you live off-campus, there are excessive amounts of bills that you don't consider when living in a dorm. Every time one gets paid, another one shows up. You and your roommates will be forever talking about money and who pays what part of what bill.
MARKETING MAJOR, ARIZONA STATE UNIVERSITY

# IT'S YOUR CHOICE!

**W**hen you move off-campus there will be no more randomly assigned roommates, and that means the choice is all yours. However, who your off-campus roommate should be is not a choice to be made on a whim after a night with your pals at the local bar. This is a choice that will affect your entire year, so think it through before you commit! Here are some things to look out for:

⭐ **Focus on Number One.** This is the time to be selfish. Look for people who share the same style living as you do. If you know your friend's boyfriend is constantly going to be in your living room and that bothers you, tell her you'd rather not live with her. If your friend chugs beer for breakfast, lunch, and dinner and you don't want your home smelling like a brewery, tell him you'd rather not live with him. Just because you decide not to live with your close friends does not mean they will stop being your friends.

⭐ **Pick a winning number.** Think it will be fun to live with fifteen of your best friends? Think again. Is this the kind of atmosphere you really want the day before you have your poli sci final?

⭐ **Don't be bullied.** If your friend insists on bringing in a roommate that you don't particularly like, you are under no obligation to agree to this. Do what feels right for you.

Keep in mind that inevitably you will probably get on each other's nerves more, but have a stronger friendship after living together.

SOCIOLOGY MAJOR, TULANE UNIVERSITY

**The more people you live with, the harder it is to get everything in order. The bills are higher and there is more stuff cluttering the apartment.**

LAW AND SOCIETY MAJOR, OBERLIN COLLEGE

*Don't live with more than two other people. Remember that you and these two other people all have girlfriends, boyfriends, and friends. Before you know it, you'll have eight people living in your house.*

TELECOMMUNICATION ARTS MAJOR, UNIVERSITY OF GEORGIA

When you choose a roommate, if you don't know her well and she seems a little "off," chances are you will find out by living with her that she is REALLY off. Go with your instincts.

**ENGLISH MAJOR, UNIVERSITY OF TEXAS—AUSTIN**

I learned that you become like those around you, and since you are usually around your roommate a lot, don't live with people you don't want to be like.

**BUSINESS MANAGEMENT MAJOR, CALIFORNIA STATE UNIVERSITY**

*I rented an apartment with my two friends, and we needed another roommate to fill the fourth bedroom. One of my roommates found a girl to join us. Turns out she was a heavy drug user, had no clue how to pay bills, could not control how much she drank, and was a slob. I had trusted my roommate to make a good choice and that was my mistake. Make sure you interview anyone who plans to live with you.*

**ELECTRICAL ENGINEERING MAJOR, TEXAS A&M UNIVERSITY**

# A PLACE TO CALL HOME: SIGNING THE LEASE

**Y**ou and your roommates have found the perfect off-campus house. Sure, the front steps are termite-ridden and the carpet is orange shag, but it's going to be your first real home on your own—as soon as you sign on the dotted line. In order to rent an off-campus apartment or house, students must sign a lease with a landlord who is not affiliated with the university. A lease is a binding, legal contract outlining the rights and responsibilities of the tenants and the landlord.

Every landlord has his own rules as to how the lease should be signed. There are usually three ways in which it is done:

1. **Only one roommate can be the primary leaseholder, with the other roommates listed as sublessees.** The primary leaseholder is solely responsible for paying the rent in full and on time, regardless of the other roommates, since the legal document is in his or her name. If one roommate doesn't pay the rent, you are the only one who is liable.

2. **You and your roommates can be co-tenants, which means you all sign one lease and share the responsibility equally.** If one person doesn't pay the rent, you are all responsible for coming up with the full amount. You also all share the legal responsibility in case of a problem.

3. **All the roommates sign separate leases.** Each person is responsible only for his share of the rent. <u>This is your best option.</u> If your roommate skips out, you still are responsible only for the rent amount listed on your lease. Landlords do not have to offer this, but you should always ask!

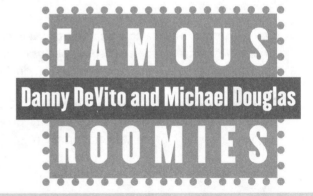

FAMOUS

Danny DeVito and Michael Douglas

ROOMIES

## STUDENTS SAY: LOOK BEFORE YOU LEASE

I recommend signing separate leases so that late rent does not affect you.

POLITICAL SCIENCE MAJOR, GEORGIA SOUTHERN UNIVERSITY

Make sure you know the penalty for having to break the lease before you commit to anything. You never know when your roommate may decide to drop out, transfer, or study abroad.

PSYCHOLOGY MAJOR, UNIVERSITY OF KENTUCKY

Cardinal rule: *Make sure your roommates can afford to live off-campus before you commit to signing a lease with them.*

JURISPRUDENCE MAJOR, AUBURN UNIVERSITY

# WHEN YOUR ROOMMATE WON'T COUGH UP THE RENT

**I**t's the first of the month and—big surprise—your roommate has gone AWOL again. Now the rent is going to be late or partially unpaid, and you are put in the uncomfortable role of bill collector. Before you repossess his scanner, here are some ideas to get him to pay up:

1. **Talk to your roommate before the situation gets out of hand.** The point of this discussion is not to humiliate your roommate, but to get the rent paid. Be tactful and to the point. Do not lay blame—just say that it's that time of the month again and you are missing his check.

2. **Approach your landlord with the problem.** She may be able to send your roommate a "reminder" letter.

3. **Bring in a neutral party to act as a mediator.** If it gets to the point where your roommate refuses to pay, many universities offer services for housing disputes.

4. **Expect the unexpected.** Your roommate is kicked out of college. Your roommate has an emergency at home and needs to take the year off. It happens. Students say it's best to think ahead to avoid having the rent bill arrive in your mailbox after your roommate is long gone, leaving you unable to cover his share.

- ▣ **Make a plan.** Agree up front with your roommate that leaving voluntarily will require 30-days' notice, and he will still have to pay his portion of the rent until he finds someone to take his place.

- ▣ **Advertise.** Help your out-the-door roommate look for a new roommate. Post signs around school and in the school newspaper.

- ▣ **The backup.** If worse comes to worst and your roommate skips out on you, ask your landlord to use the absent roommate's share of the security deposit to help pay the rent.

# STUDENTS SAY: PAY UP!

When the rent and other bills arrive, I open them immediately and post them with the return envelope on the bulletin board in our kitchen. Everyone drops her check into the envelope, and she has to do it ten days before the bill is due.

INTERNATIONAL RELATIONS MAJOR, BUCKNELL UNIVERSITY

My roommate is always late paying the rent, so I know I have to start asking him for the money no less than a week before it is due.

ENGLISH/HISTORY MAJOR, INDIANA UNIVERSITY

My roommates and I told our other roommate that if he was late with one more rent payment, we would have to kick him out of the apartment. You never want to force someone out—it's not a good feeling. But then again, it doesn't feel good either when the landlord is always calling and yelling at you over missed payments. We tried to make him understand how his neglect impacted on all of us. MATHEMATICS MAJOR, UNIVERSITY OF CALIFORNIA—DAVIS

# SHOW ME THE MONEY: PAYING THE BILLS

**Y**ou and your roommates are like peas in a pod—you all like to study in complete silence, all are a bit messy, and all like to throw a great party. But on the first and the fifteenth of every month when the stack of bills arrive, the similarities end. One roommate is diligent about paying on time, one roommate needs constant reminders, and one roommate is forever broke.

That's when the hostility and resentment begins to grow, often resulting in roommates arguing over how much to contribute or what each person's share is. Who knew that ten-minute hot showers were a true luxury?

Here are some tips to follow so that paying bills runs as smoothly as possible:

**1. Create a System for Utilities**

◎ If possible, find an apartment that includes utilities as part of the monthly rent. The fewer bills, the fewer conflicts.

◎ When it comes to heat and water bills, it is often simpler to agree to spilt these bills evenly rather than haggle over usage. Agree to turn out the lights and turn off the water when you are not using it.

◎ If you don't want the hassle of splitting each bill evenly, guesstimate the bills so that each person has close to an equal financial responsibility each month. For example, if the heating bill is $200 and the water bill is $100 and the telephone bill is $100, then one roommate is responsible for paying the first bill and the other roommate is responsible for the other two.

2. **Address questions up front.**

◎ What will happen if one of you does not have enough money to pay the rent or a utility bill one month?

◎ How will late charges be handled?

◎ Whose name will the bills be registered under?

Source: www.hfcu.org/whatsnew/hff/dec98_1.htm, "How to Handle Roommate Finances"

# STUDENTS SAY: BEWARE OF THE BENJAMINS

One roommate would turn the heat up to 80 degrees while we weren't there. Our heating bill one month was $350! I was left feeling bitter because I always felt she deserved to pay a greater share of the bill. I wish I had talked to her about turning down the heat.

ENGLISH MAJOR, CASE WESTERN RESERVE UNIVERSITY

Our neighbors elected a financial chair for the house who opened a checking account for house-specific purchases. Every semester, each of the girls put in a couple hundred dollars that they used to pay the bills and recreational expenses. If the account got low, they all chipped in a little more.

ECONOMICS MAJOR, BUCKNELL UNIVERSITY

We had a running list of extra expenses that one person or another ended up paying for—like beer for parties, cleaning supplies, etc.—and at the end of the year, the expenses were totaled and checks were written so that the financial responsibility evened out.

**POLITICAL SCIENCE MAJOR, BROWN UNIVERSITY**

**Getting everyone to claim their long-distance calls was a nightmare.** We ended up getting rid of the long distance, so people would have to call us or we would use collect calling.

JURISPRUDENCE MAJOR, AUBURN UNIVERSITY

*You should know up front that if a bill is in your name and it doesn't get paid, it will damage your credit.*

GOVERNMENT MAJOR, CONNECTICUT COLLEGE

## STUDENTS SAY: WHEN ONE ROOMMATE WON'T ANTE UP

If a bill was late because of a particular roommate, that person would have to pay all the late fees.

ENGINEERING MAJOR, GEORGIA SOUTHERN UNIVERSITY

My roommate would leave our bills in a stack and pay them a month after they were due. To try and rectify the problem, I left her notes on the fridge when each bill was due.

ENGLISH MAJOR, UNIVERSITY OF TEXAS—AUSTIN

It's better to have a quick, uncomfortable conversation about bills and money than to have a series of heated, difficult conversations later on.

WOMEN'S STUDIES MAJOR, SMITH COLLEGE

# STUDENTS SAY: YOU GET THE TABLE, I GET THE CHAIR

Some off-campus apartments come with furniture included, but many do not. What happens when one room-mate is happy with an overturned box as a coffee table and a couch with the stuffing hanging out and the other prefers coordinating birch furniture from Ikea with matching slipcovers? Here are some issues that students faced:

**Make sure you keep all your receipts for furniture and write every-thing down, so at the end of the year you have a record of what the item costs and how much each person contributed.**

CHEMISTRY MAJOR, UNIVERSITY OF THE PACIFIC

**Large purchases like furniture are difficult to divide because the question of who gets to keep the shared purchase inevitably comes up at the end of the year. I avoided this by just buying the whole thing myself or letting my roommate buy it.**

POLITICAL SCIENCE MAJOR, PENNSYLVANIA STATE UNIVERSITY

If we had to buy furniture for our apartment, we would split the money evenly, then at the end of the year if someone wanted to buy it, they could—or we would try to sell it and split the money.

ENVIRONMENTAL STUDIES MAJOR, UNIVERSITY OF COLORADO—BOULDER

Five of us lived together in a house after freshman year. We pooled everything left in our parents' homes—old sofas, broken chairs, cracked plates. The place was bursting with remnants of our attics at home.

ECONOMICS MAJOR, UNIVERSITY OF NORTH CAROLINA

# STUDENTS SAY: THE LIST GOES ON

We've covered the big apartment issues you might face with your roommate, but what about all the little day-to-day stuff? Read on to be prepared:

The need to borrow a car increases when one lives off-campus. Make some sort of arrangement to borrow your roommate's car but make sure that you are respectful and you offer to pay for the gas and repairs.

**POLITICAL SCIENCE MAJOR, WASHINGTON UNIVERSITY—ST. LOUIS**

If you are a big TV watcher, you should get your own TV for your bedroom. There is no chance that you and your roommate will always want to watch all the same shows.

**JOURNALISM MAJOR, OHIO UNIVERSITY**

*The trash was an issue. In a dorm, you just have to drag it down the hall. In a house, you have to go outside and bring it to the curb on certain days. We had to assign everyone a week to do this or our place got disgusting.*

**BIOLOGY MAJOR, JOHNS HOPKINS UNIVERSITY**

When you live in a place with a dishwasher, it's so exciting. But most people don't realize that the clean dishes don't put themselves back in the cupboard. Nobody ever unloaded our dishwasher so we never had plates to eat off.

SOCIOLOGY MAJOR, PENNSYLVANIA STATE UNIVERSITY

**When we moved off-campus, all my roommates agreed to buy a puppy. My advice—never get a puppy in the winter, two weeks before finals, that needs to be housebroken and walked constantly, because none of you will want to be responsible for it!**

ENGLISH MAJOR, TUFTS UNIVERSITY

**You and your roommate(s) have found a way to happily call your off-campus digs home sweet home,** which is good, because it's time to turn our attention to a more serious subject. There will be times when your roommate needs you—not to drive him to class or to lend her some money—but to help when something is seriously wrong. How do you handle when your roommate has an eating disorder, is lonely, or abuses alcohol? The next chapter will guide you in the right direction.

# 9 WHEN YOUR ROOMMATE NEEDS HELP

*Sometimes you have to remember that schoolwork can wait and that you need to sit down with your roommate and a mug of hot chocolate <u>now</u>.*

**CLASSICAL STUDIES MAJOR, UNIVERSITY OF PENNSYLVANIA**

# Overall, for most students college is a fairly carefree and happy time

(all tests, papers, and projects aside). For some students, though, problems arise that make dealing with life a little more difficult than it is for the average person. Such problems may range from homesickness to clinical depression, from being dumped by a significant other to being sexually abused, from an illness to a death in the family.

When your roommate is struggling, it is a safe bet that you will be one of the first to know. What do you do with this knowledge? How do you help? This chapter will show you the right way to deal.

**O**ne of the signs that you are a good roommate is being able to confront your roommate about a potentially harmful problem. It takes courage to show you care and are concerned. It also helps to handle the problem in an appropriate manner. Whatever the nature of the problem, keep the following advice in mind when approaching your roommate:

➡ **Keep it one-on-one.** Ask to talk to your roommate in private. The idea is to lessen the embarrassment and not make your roommate defensive.

➡ **Be direct and honest.** Acknowledge that you are aware there is a problem. Explain that you are concerned and are willing to aid your roommate in finding help.

➡ **Describe your observations.** If your roommate has been acting strange or inappropriate, tell her what you have observed in a non-judgmental manner.

➡ **Listen carefully.** Try not to agree or disagree. Stay neutral.

➤ **Offer a recommendation.** Tell him where to find professional help. Point out that campus services are nearby and free. Offer to go with him.

➤ **Be patient.** At first your roommate may not identify the situation as a problem, or may feel embarrassed or threatened by your concern. Be consistent with your support.

➤ **You can't do it all.** Realize that it is ultimately your roommate's choice to seek help. No amount of pleading, begging, or preaching by you will make someone do something he doesn't want to do.

Dropping subtle hints does not work. It is best to address issues head on.

MECHANICAL ENGINEERING MAJOR, UNIVERSITY OF MICHIGAN

# Most people resist change when they feel like they are being forced into a conversation or put on the defensive.

ENGLISH LITERATURE MAJOR, COLORADO COLLEGE

*Remember, you are just a college student. Some things are way too big for one person to solve. If the problem is serious, seek outside (professional) help right away.*

POLITICAL SCIENCE MAJOR, UNIVERSITY OF CALIFORNIA—BERKELEY

# HOMESICKNESS/LONELINESS

**Think you're the only one who misses your high school friends, your little sister stealing your clothes, or your mom's apple pie?** Think again. Most students experience homesickness at some point during college—but with a little help from you, it will usually go away! Here's what you can do:

★ **Include him in your activities.** Getting your roommate involved in a club or an intramural sport forces him to leave the room and make new friends.

★ **Suggest that you and your roommate eat dinner together certain nights of the week.** Invite other people from your floor to join you.

★ **Make your own memories.** Is he always talking about the fun times he had with his friends back home? Go out and have fun or be silly together and then she will be telling her friends back home about the good times that the two of you are having.

My roommate was lonely being away from home, and I would help by listening to her talk about home.

LAW MAJOR, ALBANY LAW SCHOOL

*When one of us got lonely, we'd hit the bars to meet guys. By the next morning, there was enough new drama to forget about being homesick!*

ANTHROPOLOGY MAJOR, KENT STATE UNIVERSITY

**When my roommate was homesick, I tried to make him laugh. A lighthearted approach can often better contextualize things.**

ENGLISH MAJOR, UNIVERSITY OF CALIFORNIA—DAVIS

# DEPRESSION

**Your roommate is seriously bummed out.** Maybe her parents are getting a divorce, maybe he's failing his classes—whatever the reason, depression is very common among college students who are living on their own for the first time. Depression is treatable; however, many people don't seek help because they don't realize that they are clinically depressed. Other people see depression as a sign of weakness and don't want to reach out for help. Here are some symptoms to look for:

- ☑ persistent sad, anxious, or "empty" demeanor

- ☑ feelings of hopelessness, pessimism, guilt, and worthlessness

- ☑ loss of interest or pleasure in ordinary activities

- ☑ sleep disturbances (i.e., insomnia or oversleeping)

- ☑ eating disturbances (i.e., increased or decreased appetite or weight)

◼ decreased energy, fatigue, or feeling "slowed down"

◼ thoughts of death or suicide; suicide attempts

◼ difficulty concentrating, remembering, and making decisions

Source: www.nimh.nih.gov The National Institute of Mental Health "What do these Students Have in Common?"

# THE DOS AND DON'TS OF HELPING A DEPRESSED ROOMMATE

**<u>DO:</u>**

➤ Be supportive and listen.

➤ Engage him in activities and conversation.

➤ Tell your roommate if his behavior frightens you.

➤ Encourage him to get treatment. If he won't see a mental health professional, you should see one yourself to gain better insight on the situation.

➤ Take any talk of suicide or attempts seriously. Even if you think your friend did it or said something just to get attention, call your school's suicide emergency hotline or call 911.

## DON'T:

➤ Feel that you are responsible for your roommate's depression.

➤ Think that you'll be able to fix her life or quickly change her mood. Don't try to talk her out of her depression.

➤ Deny or minimize your roommate's pain. Depression is a real problem. Your roommate needs your support.

Source: www.nimh.nih.gov The National Institute of Mental Health "What do these Students Have in Common?"

# STUDENTS SAY: HELP A DEPRESSED FRIEND

One of my roommates was severely depressed throughout college. It got so bad that I brought her to student counseling. She fought me at the beginning, but to this day, she thanks me for helping her to face her issues with a professional.

POLITICAL SCIENCE MAJOR, WASHINGTON UNIVERSITY—ST. LOUIS

When my roommate was depressed, I left phone numbers for help lines all around our room. I didn't feel close enough to talk to him about it, so I told his best friend what was going on.

POLITICAL ECONOMY MAJOR, TULANE UNIVERSITY

*My roommate was depressed, and I told her about the university's counseling. She was surprised to find out that it was free. I went with her to her first appointment.*

ECONOMICS MAJOR, UNIVERSITY OF NORTH CAROLINA—CHAPEL HILL

**A**norexia and bulimia are both serious eating disorders. People develop eating disorders as a way of dealing with the stresses and pressures of life—often it is a way to exercise control when the rest of life seems out of control.

What is **anorexia**? It is self-imposed starvation. Students with anorexia tend to be obsessed with food yet constantly deny their hunger. Warning signs of anorexia may be if your roommate:

◎ Is thin and keeps losing weight

◎ Obsessively diets even though she is already thin

◎ Has a distorted body image (i.e., sees herself as fat even though she isn't)

◎ Exercises all the time

◎ Weighs herself several times a day

◎ Says she feels chilled even though the temperature is warm

◎ Begins to lose her hair

**W**hat is **bulimia? It is a cycle of out-of-control eating followed by purging (vomiting or excessive use of laxatives or diuretics).** Warning signs of bulimia may be if your roommate:

✴ Binge eats

✴ Goes to the bathroom frequently after meals

✴ Develops swollen glands

✴ Appears to go up and down in weight

Adapted from: www.felician.edu/health_counseling/

# THE DOS AND DON'TS OF HELPING A ROOMMATE THROUGH AN EATING DISORDER

## DO:

★ Explain that you are concerned. Give specific examples of behavior that concerned you.

★ Realize that it may take more than one approach before she will agree to get help. Don't give up!

★ Approach the situation in a friendly, laid-back manner. Don't sound as if your mission is to rescue her or save her.

## DON'T:

★ Make your roommate feel ashamed or guilty. Do not use "you" statements like, "you just need to eat." Instead use "I" statements, like "I'm concerned because you refuse to eat," or "It makes me worried to hear you vomiting so often."

★ Give simple solutions. For example, "Why don't you just start eating again?" Eating disorders are not simple problems with simple remedies.

★ Initiate or participate in conversations about weight and food. When she asks you if she looks fat, don't get sucked in and answer. This legitimizes the topic. Instead, ask why she feels this is important.

★ Try to force her to eat or tempt her with goodies. Eating disorders have nothing to do with food.

★ Compare her to other students. Avoid saying someone is "thin" or "obese."

★ Take on her problem as your own problem. Don't agree to hide her eating disorder. Don't try to become her therapist or make life overly easy for her—this just makes it easier for her to hide from her problems.

★ Expect her to get better overnight. Eating disorders are complex syndromes with many causes. It takes a long time to recover.

Source: www.nationaleatingdisorders.org and www.hedc.org

## STUDENTS SAY: BE THERE WITH SUPPORT

Sophomore year one of my roommates was bulimic. My other roommates and I had an intervention and told her we were really worried about her. We agreed to go to a counselor with her and sit there the whole time. We used our student health services and they were great. She is now doing a million times better.

CLASSICS MAJOR, UNIVERSITY OF CALIFORNIA—SANTA BARBARA

My roommate was anorexic. I tried to be available and approachable, without being intrusive. Never be overly critical or forceful. Be a roommate and a friend and leave the actual "treatment" to a trained professional.

SPANISH MAJOR, YALE UNIVERSITY

My roommate confronted me about my eating disorder in a way that made me feel guilty and defensive. I wish she had done it in a nicer, gentler way. It was never the same between us after that.

ENGLISH LITERATURE MAJOR, COLORADO COLLEGE

My roommate was bulimic but she was not willing to confront or talk about the issue with me. Since we were not particularly close, I went and talked to one of her good friends about it, hoping she would respond better to someone she trusted on a deeper level.

INTEGRATED MARKETING MAJOR, EMERSON COLLEGE

# ALCOHOL ABUSE

**M**ost college students—especially freshmen—do not fully understand the effects of alcohol, and many wind up going too far. Here are some signs of alcohol abuse:

- ◼ Missing classes and failing to complete assignments because of drinking

- ◼ Noticeable changes in mood and behavior

- ◼ Becoming angry and violent when drinking

- ◼ Drinking alone

- ◼ Drinking to escape problems or stressful situations

- ◼ Continuing to drink even after previously getting in trouble due to alcohol consumption

If you recognize any of these signs in your roommate, you should try to get help.

## Do:

- Let your roommate know you are genuinely concerned and offer to go with him to student health services.

- Be prepared to face resistance. If this happens, leave a telephone number to call for help on your roommate's desk or bed.

## Don't:

- Tell yourself it's just a phase your roommate is going through or that lots of college kids drink a lot. Ignoring it won't make it go away.

- Beat around the bush when discussing your concern.

- Believe that you alone can change your roommate's drinking habits.

Source: www.bc.edu/offices/bcpd/prevention/alcohol/ and www.colby.edu/health.serv/drugs/friend.html

# STUDENTS SAY: WHEN DRINKING IS OUT OF CONTROL

My sophomore roommate was an alcoholic. She would go off and drink by herself when she was feeling down. I tried to talk to her about it and be her friend, but she ultimately had to move home and get help.

ACCOUNTING MAJOR, CAPITAL UNIVERSITY

I thought my roommate was drinking too much and neglecting her studies. Instead of saying anything, I began inviting her to study with me. I made studying a fun thing to do together and this worked really well.

POLITICAL SCIENCE MAJOR, VANDERBILT UNIVERSITY

*My roommate and three other friends confronted my drinking problem by having an intervention. I had hit rock bottom. They saved my college career . . . they saved my life.*

PUBLIC RELATIONS MAJOR, MOUNT MERCY COLLEGE

**If your roommate comes to you and tells you that she has been sexually assaulted or abused, the answer is not to immediately hunt down the slime that did this.** Instead, take the following approach:

### Do:

◎ Tell your roommate it was <u>not her fault</u>. Most people blame themselves for what happened.

◎ Let your roommate choose whether or not to report the assault. It is her choice. You should be supportive of her decision. However, you should advise your roommate that in order to keep that option open, she should keep all evidence. This means not showering or brushing teeth. The clothes she was wearing should be kept in a paper bag.

◎ Encourage your roommate to get support and counseling.

**Don't:**

◎ Hug or touch your roommate to offer support without asking first. Remember, she was just violated and you don't want to re-traumatize her.

◎ Ask questions that begin with "why?" You don't want to sound judgmental.

◎ Judge. No matter what your roommate was drinking or wearing, it was not her fault.

◎ Pressure. Let your roommate share only whatever details she is comfortable with.

Source: www.spectrum.trotst.edu/~save/helping-afriend.htm

# STUDENTS SAY: DEALING WITH DEATH IS DIFFICULT

Death is a fact of life, but that does not make it any easier when it happens to someone we love. Students tell how they helped to comfort their roommates during a time of sorrow:

My freshman roommate's mother had died six months prior to college. It was very difficult talking to her about her mom because it broke my heart. I wanted to do whatever I could to "fix" her, but the only way to do that was to listen and just be there for her.

SCIENCE MAJOR, PURDUE UNIVERSITY

# When I had a family member die, my roommate gave me compassionate distance, which I needed.

**ELECTRICAL ENGINEERING MAJOR, UNIVERSITY OF LOUISVILLE**

My roommate's close high school friend was killed in a car accident and she took the death hard. I tried to offer encouraging words that might help her accept the reality of it and continue on with her own life instead of dwelling on what had happened to her friend.

**INTERNATIONAL RELATIONS MAJOR, LELAND STANFORD JUNIOR UNIVERSITY**

# STUDENTS SAY: WHEN YOUR ROOMMATE IS SICK

It may be a broken bone. It may be a horrible virus. It may just be a cold. Whatever the illness or injury, roommates often turn to roommates in times of sickness (kind of like marriage—"in sickness and in health"!) Here's what students say helps:

One of my roommates had a seizure disorder, but he hid that fact from us. Then he had a seizure our sophomore year. We called the police and spent almost 24 hours in a state of panic. It would have been better if he had told us this might happen.

HISTORY MAJOR, BOSTON COLLEGE

My roommate once became seriously ill. I called an emergency room and got a cab to take us both there. I then contacted her parents and let them know about the situation. They came and took over later that night.

BIOLOGY MAJOR, SMITH COLLEGE

*When my roommate had mono, I would bring him soup every day until he was able to function properly again.*

JOURNALISM MAJOR, SYRACUSE UNIVERSITY

## STUDENTS SAY: I'LL BE THERE

You never know what problem may befall your roommate. Students say the best prescription is a little TLC and lots of support:

My roommate had credit card debt up to her eyeballs, which gave her frequent panic attacks. I was taking a massage class at the height of her anxiety, so I would give her massages to help her relieve stress.

PHILOSOPHY MAJOR, ANTIOCH COLLEGE

My roommate was cut from every sorority during rush. Almost everyone on our hall had pledged, and she felt very left out and very rejected. I tried to be around a lot and not make a big deal out of my sorority functions. I also tried to casually include her in activities with my new Greek friends.

HISTORY MAJOR, WAKE FOREST UNIVERSITY

My roommate decided to have an abortion. She had her mind set on it, so I supported her. I went with her to the appointment, took care of her afterward, and lied to everyone when people asked what was wrong with her.

PRE-LAW MAJOR, UNIVERSITY OF SOUTH CAROLINA

My roommate would have panic attacks and get really stressed about school. She always thought she wasn't doing well. Hanging out and talking about it always helped her calm down and feel better.

BUSINESS MAJOR, UNIVERSITY OF TEXAS—AUSTIN

# Granted, bad things <u>do</u> happen, but just as you are there for your roommate,

campus health services are always there for guidance, support, and medical assistance. But what if the only thing wrong with your roommate is that he's just downright mean and nasty? Turn the page to read about roommate horror stories!

# 10 TALES FROM THE TORMENTED

*My roommate constantly forgot to flush the toilet.*

FINANCE MAJOR, UNIVERSITY OF HOUSTON

## Let's face it, it happens. You can get stuck with a really (and we mean <u>really</u>!) bad roommate.

Some students, no matter how masterful their conflict resolution skills, are paired with a roommate so horrible that they long for a magic wand that will make their roommate disappear. You think you've had problems with your roommate? Read on for truly terrifying tales from the tormented—and the tormentors!

# Puked on my bed.

ECONOMICS MAJOR, UNIVERSITY OF NORTH CAROLINA

## Left me owing over $400 in unpaid rent and utility bills.

FINANCE MAJOR, UNIVERSITY OF MICHIGAN—ANN ARBOR

## *Ate fried chicken while typing on my laptop.*

CREATIVE WRITING MAJOR, EMORY UNIVERSITY

## STUDENTS SAY:
THE WORST THING MY ROOMMATE EVER DID WAS . . .

**Peed on our floor when he was drunk.**

FINANCE/COMMUNICATIONS MAJOR, UNIVERSITY OF SOUTH FLORIDA

**Stole one of my term papers and handed it in as his own.**

HISTORY MAJOR, COLUMBIA UNIVERSITY

*Wrecked my car and refused to pay for it.*

CLASSICS MAJOR, UNIVERSITY OF CALIFORNIA—SANTA BARBARA

Brushed his teeth repeatedly with my toothbrush after I asked him a number of times to stop.

LITERATURE MAJOR, UNIVERSITY OF NOTRE DAME

Had a major party the night before a major exam after specifically agreeing not to.

COMMUNICATIONS MAJOR, SEATTLE UNIVERSITY

Had sex in my bed.

ENGLISH MAJOR, ROANOKE COLLEGE

# Brewed her own beer in our room!

ENGLISH/HISTORY MAJOR, CARNEGIE MELLON UNIVERSITY

Invited thirty people to our room to watch porn tapes. Gross!

COMMUNICATIONS MAJOR, TEXAS STATE UNIVERSITY—SAN MARCOS

# THE WORST THING I EVER DID TO MY ROOMMATE WAS . . .

Punch him in a very sensitive place.

POLITICAL SCIENCE MAJOR, VILLANOVA UNIVERSITY

## Fart and make the room stink . . . on a regular basis.

TRAVEL INDUSTRY MANAGEMENT MAJOR, UNIVERSITY OF HAWAII

*Trash his room*—there were crickets, ketchup, mustard, and buckets of water involved.

JURISPRUDENCE MAJOR, AUBURN UNIVERSITY

## Drink all of her vodka and fill the bottle with water.

PSYCHOLOGY MAJOR, UNIVERSITY OF PENNSYLVANIA

**STUDENTS SAY:**
THE WORST THING I EVER DID TO MY ROOMMATE WAS . . .

Go a whole year without ever buying milk, yet I ate at least one bowl of milk-covered cereal every day. You do the math.

ENGLISH MAJOR, RICKS COLLEGE

Have a party in the house we shared and didn't invite her.

CRIMINAL JUSTICE MAJOR, UNIVERSITY OF NEVADA

*Convince his girlfriend to break up with him.*

HISTORY MAJOR, COLUMBIA UNIVERSITY

My roommate did not wake me up for my first chemistry exam even though she was in my class, and then she lied to others when they asked where I was.

**BUSINESS MAJOR, CONCORDIA COLLEGE**

**My roommate wrote a mean English paper about me accusing me of horrible things that weren't true, and she read it out loud in class.**

**COMMUNICATIONS MAJOR, AMERICAN UNIVERSITY**

# STUDENTS SAY: ALL'S FAIR IN LOVE AND WAR

When my roommate took off all her clothes in front of my current boyfriend, I was pretty pissed.

COMMUNICATIONS MAJOR, CONCORDIA COLLEGE

My roommate kissed the boy she knew I was in love with and she didn't even like him.

ENGLISH MAJOR, VILLANOVA UNIVERSITY

*My boyfriend thought I was a virgin, and my roommate told him that I had sex with another guy before him.*

MARKETING MAJOR, ARIZONA STATE UNIVERSITY

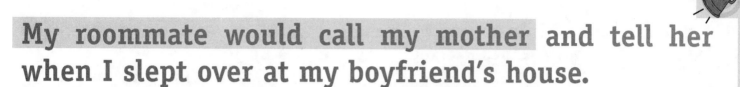

My roommate would call my mother and tell her when I slept over at my boyfriend's house.

FINANCE MAJOR, GEORGETOWN UNIVERSITY

I told my roommate's boyfriend she was cheating on him. Hey, she was!

SOCIOLOGY MAJOR, UNIVERSITY OF ARIZONA

## STUDENTS SAY: INQUIRING MINDS HAVE TO SNOOP

I liked to secretly check my roommate's email because we never really talked much and I wanted to see what she was up to.

SOCIOLOGY MAJOR, MESSIAH COLLEGE

I once read a very personal letter from my roommate's boyfriend because I just knew it would be dirty!

RELIGIOUS STUDIES MAJOR, ARIZONA STATE UNIVERSITY

*Even though you may live with someone for an extended period of time, your roommates still have their secrets. Never assume you are friends just because you share the same air.*

LATIN AMERICAN STUDIES MAJOR, WELLESLEY COLLEGE

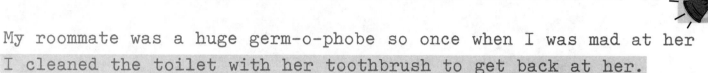

# STUDENTS SAY: REVENGE MADE ME DO IT

My roommate was a huge germ-o-phobe so once when I was mad at her I cleaned the toilet with her toothbrush to get back at her.

**POLITICAL SCIENCE MAJOR, MARY WASHINGTON COLLEGE**

She took my name off the answering machine because I accidentally erased her message.

**CHEMISTRY MAJOR, GEORGIA SOUTHERN UNIVERSITY**

*My roommate's boyfriend called our room at four in the morning to tell her that he missed her. I was so angry he woke me up that I told him never to call again and hung up the phone.*

**GOVERNMENT MAJOR, CONNECTICUT COLLEGE**

# If My Roommate Dies, I Get an Automatic 4.0!

If you have fantasies of offing your roommate and figure your GPA will benefit as well, think again. One of the biggest urban legends circulating on college campuses is that if your roommate dies, you automatically get a 4.0 for the semester. We don't know where this rumor began, but it has never, ever been proven true—and we doubt you'll be the first one to make it happen!

**T**here will be times when you are going to out-and-out hate your roommate. And, you know what? That's okay. Conflict is a fact of life. In fact, that's healthy as long as you know how to fight fair:

1. **Talk it out.** Air your grievances. The silent treatment never works. Bottling up emotions in order to keep the peace will result in an explosion that could rival Mount St. Helens.

2. **See it from the other side.** Try to understand where your roommate is coming from. Remember, your way is not the only way.

3. **Say you're sorry.** Be the bigger person and initiate the resolution. Even if you still don't agree with your roommate, be the first to say (in a nice way) "I'm sorry that you feel that way," or "I'm sorry if I offended you."

4. **Express your emotions.** It is very difficult for your roommate to argue with your emotions. For example, if you say "I feel very uncomfortable when you have sex with your boyfriend while I'm still in the room," your roommate can't counter with "No you don't." She'll have no choice but to understand.

5. **Control your anger.** If you feel yourself saying things in anger that you will later regret, walk away. Save the conversation for a time when you can be rational.

## STUDENTS SAY: DON'T LET IT FESTER

My roommate and I never had to compromise because most of our issues were never brought up—we just fumed about each other and vented to friends. Things never got better between us.

ECONOMICS MAJOR, INDIANA UNIVERSITY

If I do something that annoys or offends my roommate, and she is tight-lipped about it, if I repeat the behavior unknowingly, she has no right being mad at me for something she didn't say!

CRIMINAL JUSTICE MAJOR, STATE UNIVERSITY OF NEW YORK—ALBANY

I think that sometimes I was way too kind to the people I lived with. If you are going to stay sane in college, you have to know when it's time to stand up for yourself.

SOCIOLOGY MAJOR, NEW YORK UNIVERSITY

# CALLING IT QUITS

**F**or whatever reason, you simply were not put on this earth to share a confined space with your current roommate. When is it time to raise the white flag and call it quits?

1. **Recognize a toxic relationship.** Is your roommate situation stressing you out so much that you are having physical symptoms such as headaches, stomachaches, or problems sleeping? Do you dread being in your dorm room? These are all signs of a roommate relationship that's in serious trouble.

2. **Hold out for the thirty-day trial period.** Before you go racing to the housing office, understand that most housing departments won't even consider a roommate change (especially for freshmen) the first month of school. Conventional wisdom says you should wait until you have lived together for more than a month to make sure that the problems aren't intertwined with the adjustment to school and new classes.

3. **Consider the alternatives.** Some universities' dorms are overcrowded and there may not be the space available at that moment to make a switch. Plus, you may not like your new roommate any better than your current roommate.

4. **Seek help.** Make sure you've attempted mediation with a neutral third party. A negotiator—whether it's your RA or a common, trusted friend—can often find a solution that neither of you can see behind your wall of anger.

## A WORD TO THE WISE:

If you are truly miserable, *be proactive*. You don't need to be a prisoner for the next nine months. Many things that create stress in our lives are beyond our control—this is not.

## STUDENTS SAY: SEE YOU LATER, ALLIGATOR

**There is a time to just give up.** Sometimes you can't make it work—even with the best effort.

THEATER MAJOR, NEW YORK UNIVERSITY

You don't always realize how bad the situation is until you stand back and gain some perspective on the situation. Your living conditions affect every aspect of your life.

CHEMICAL ENGINEERING MAJOR, COOPER UNION

*Everybody has bad days, but if you feel that living with your room-mate causes a bad day every day—move out!*

ORGANIZATIONAL COMMUNICATIONS MAJOR, LIPSCOMB UNIVERSITY

# STUDENTS SAY: THE BEHIND-THE-BACK MOVE

Sure, it's going to be difficult to tell your roommate that you're leaving. (In fact, the majority of the students we asked said that the most difficult conversation they ever had was telling their roommate they no longer wanted to live with them!) The answer is not to avoid the situation until you're already gone. Here's what students had to say on the subject:

My roommate never said a complaining word to me. Then one day my RA called me to a meeting to discuss her moving out, because I stay up too late and she can't sleep. I was completely unprepared and dumbfounded. I just wish she could have come to me in the first place instead of going behind my back.
**CRIMINAL JUSTICE MAJOR, GEORGE WASHINGTON UNIVERSITY**

*The worst thing I ever did was move out of my dorm room without discussing it with my roommate. I couldn't afford the housing anymore and had to find a less expensive place to live, but I was embarrassed to tell her so I took the easy way out and just left. I wound up feeling guilty for weeks.*
**INTERNATIONAL RELATIONS MAJOR, LELAND STANFORD JUNIOR UNIVERSITY**

## Sure, there are plenty of roommate horror stories out there—but don't despair.

For as many bad roommate tales there are in this chapter, there are twice as many great roommate stories out there. Read on for some warm and fuzzy roommate experiences.

# 11 ROOMMATE BLISS AND BEYOND

*My roommate consoled me when I was lonely, made me laugh when I was sad, and supported me in my decisions. I wouldn't have made it through the first year without her.*

POLITICAL SCIENCE MAJOR, WESTMONT COLLEGE

# Some students are lucky enough to look across their dorm room or apartment

and thank the Housing God for giving them the best roommate in the world. So how did these fortunate students get so lucky? Some roommates report that it just "clicked" that first day of school, while other roommates had to work at their relationship, developing a close-knit friendship forged from obstacles. And then there are those easy-going folks who just "loved the one they're with" and enjoyed the roommate experience year after year, no matter with whom they shared their air.

Whatever the reason, when the roommate relationship works, it can be one of the richest, most educational, and fun experiences of your lifetime—just ask the students featured in this chapter!

My roommates were always there to support me. They all came to see the plays I worked on, even though theater wasn't their thing. They really showed me they cared by letting me know they respected what I did.

THEATER MAJOR, DREW UNIVERSITY

My roommate's mother called me out of the blue one day to say thank you. She cried on the phone and said I touched her daughter's life. She wanted to ensure that I knew what a profound influence I had on her daughter and how she was a much happier person for having lived with me. I cannot verbalize how much this meant to me.

GOVERNMENT MAJOR, GEORGETOWN UNIVERSITY

My roommate was there for advice without judgment when it was desperately needed.

ENGLISH MAJOR, VILLANOVA UNIVERSITY

My roommate used to make posters that would list the reasons she liked living with me. She would surprise me by putting them up when I had a big test or broke up with someone.

INTERNATIONAL COMMUNICATIONS MAJOR, TEXAS CHRISTIAN UNIVERSITY

*Whenever I would break up with a guy, my roommate would always offer to help me get revenge. I never took her up on her offers, but it was sweet to know that if I ever needed to go psycho on a guy, she would be there ready to join in.*

POLITICAL SCIENCE MAJOR, UNIVERSITY OF WISCONSIN—MADISON

*Remembered that I had two exams and woke me up because he realized that I had overslept.*

PSYCHOLOGY MAJOR, RUTGERS UNIVERSITY

**Drove me home—six hours away—when my grandma died.**

ADVERTISING MAJOR, MICHIGAN STATE UNIVERSITY

Helped me pay part of my rent because my financial aid check was two weeks late.

INTERNATIONAL RELATIONS MAJOR, SAN FRANCISCO STATE UNIVERSITY

**STUDENTS SAY:**
THE BEST THING MY ROOMMATE EVER DID FOR ME WAS . . .

Woke up all of his football teammates to stand up for me during an altercation at a bar.

GERMAN MAJOR, TULANE UNIVERSITY

Told my boyfriend a million amazing things he could do for me for Valentine's Day . . . and he listened.

SOCIOLOGY MAJOR, RUTGERS UNIVERSITY

*Stayed up all night to help me finish a project.*
BUSINESS MANAGEMENT MAJOR, CALIFORNIA STATE UNIVERSITY—FULLERTON

Covered for me when the other "girlfriend" stopped by.

ENGLISH MAJOR, UNIVERSITY OF WISCONSIN—MADISON

Brought me food when I was pulling an all-nighter.

TELECOMMUNICATIONS MAJOR, INDIANA UNIVERSITY

Break up with her boyfriend for her.

SPANISH MAJOR, UNIVERSITY OF KANSAS

Drive an hour and a half to bail her out of jail.

COMMUNICATIONS MAJOR, COLLEGE OF CHARLESTON

*Send her huge care packages when she was studying overseas and having a horrible time.*

MARKETING MAJOR, EMERSON COLLEGE

**Not ask her for the utility and rent money. I knew she was having huge financial problems and it was a one-time thing, so I just let it go.**

ENGLISH MAJOR, UNIVERSITY OF CALIFORNIA—SANTA BARBARA

**Make sure he got home safely after a rough night of partying.**

MATHEMATICS MAJOR, WESTERN ILLINOIS UNIVERSITY

Take notes for her in the class we had together because she always fell asleep during the lecture.

ENGLISH MAJOR, UNIVERSITY OF TEXAS—AUSTIN

# STUDENTS SAY: A WHOLE NEW WORLD

College is a beginning in many ways. Socially and emotionally, it's a time to take a look at life up until now (yes, we mean those painful high school years!) and decide what your next steps will be. And there's no better person to show you a new direction than a trusted roommate.

**My roommate brought me out of my shell so much.** She made a huge impact on my life and has changed the way I think about so many things. I was lucky to have been assigned to her.

**PSYCHOLOGY MAJOR, BARNARD COLLEGE**

## My roommate got me to loosen up and have fun. We became like sisters.

**JOURNALISM MAJOR, UNIVERSITY OF SOUTH CAROLINA**

My roommate gave me confidence to try things at college I had never done before. It was great to know that he was a friend who was always watching my back.

**ENGINEERING MAJOR, RENSSELAER POLYTECHNIC INSTITUTE**

# STUDENTS SAY: IT'S THE LITTLE THINGS THAT COUNT

The majority of students told us that it's the little everyday things—such as a surprise cleaning of the room or a ride onto campus in the snow—that really bring a smile to a roommate's face. Here are a few more small tokens of appreciation that netted big results for college roommates:

My roommate made a big deal about my birthday freshman year in college—my first birthday away from home. That was definitely great.

GOVERNMENT MAJOR, DARTMOUTH COLLEGE

My roommate cooked me dinner unexpectedly after a hard day of work.

SPANISH MAJOR, WILLAMETTE UNIVERSITY

My roommate took care of me when I wasn't feeling well.

ENGLISH MAJOR, CARNEGIE MELLON UNIVERSITY

After I finished my Honors thesis, my roommates got together and bought bottles of champagne and decorated the apartment to celebrate.

POLITICAL SCIENCE MAJOR, WASHINGTON UNIVERSITY—ST. LOUIS

*My roommate ran out and bought me a corsage for a formal when the guy I was going with forgot. She didn't want me to be the only one there without one!*

INDUSTRIAL AND LABOR RELATIONS MAJOR, CORNELL UNIVERSITY

You probably have had fantasies about the day you get your own room—no more smelly socks that aren't yours, no more listening to other people's bad music, no more crawling around in the dark trying to find your bed while your roommate snores peacefully. But when that day comes, we guarantee that many of you are going to miss your roommate experience, just like these students did:

**It is nice to have someone to talk to. This year I am living alone, and sometimes I get lonely.**

PSYCHOLOGY MAJOR, UNIVERSITY OF MINNESOTA

The best thing about having a roommate is the random nights we ordered pizza, watched a movie, and caught up on each other's lives. I missed that when I lived alone.

COMMUNICATIONS MAJOR, VIRGINIA POLYTECHNIC INSTITUTE AND STATE UNIVERSITY

**It's great to have roommates! Without them, there's little chance for spontaneous fun.**

HISTORY MAJOR, WILLAMETTE UNIVERSITY

Sometimes you take for granted how amazing your roommate really is until you fill out a survey on roommates that forces you to remember all the wonderful things she's done.

GOVERNMENT MAJOR, CORNELL UNIVERSITY

# ROOMMATES ARE GREAT BECAUSE THEY'LL . . .

Always find funny things to say about your ex-boyfriend, have bloody Marys with you on Sunday mornings, and taste your experimental vegan cooking!

ANTHROPOLOGY MAJOR, UNIVERSITY OF ARIZONA

## Go with you to get a piercing or a tattoo—and get one too.

ENGLISH MAJOR, CASE WESTERN RESERVE UNIVERSITY

*Know exactly when you need to talk and when the best cure is a chocolate bar.*

ART MAJOR, SKIDMORE COLLEGE

## Be a good listener, a thoughtful proofreader of your term papers, and a great assessor of fashion blunders.

HISTORY MAJOR, GEORGETOWN UNIVERSITY

# CONCLUSION

**I**t was the best of times . . . it was the worst of times . . . it will be a time that you will forever remember. Sharing a room with a stranger or a friend certainly has its ups and downs, and there is certainly no foolproof connect-the-dot formula that works for everyone. However, students who have netted fabulous friendships as a result of living with someone have given us the short-and-sweet of what to do to make it work out great with your roommate:

1. **Give compliments.** Tell her if you like her new jeans. Tell him if he played awesome at the pick-up basketball game. Everyone likes a compliment.

2. **Be happy.** Act friendly. Be pleasant to be around. Smile. Happiness breeds happiness.

3. **Laugh.** Use humor to get your points across. Make a joke about all the dirty laundry piled on the floor. Humor is non-threatening and won't make your roommate defensive.

4. **Set the ground rules early.** Make rules together and stick by them.

5. **Be respectful.** Don't criticize your roommate. Respect his right to make choices. Respect his belongings and his space.

6. **Listen.** You roommate is a person like you and often needs someone to listen to her. Lend your ears.

7. **Talk.** Don't be passive aggressive—it breeds hostility. Work together to find solutions and compromises.

8. **Don't take it personally.** Maybe he's stressed. Maybe she's tired. There will be days when your roommate is moody, cranky, or unreasonable. Let it pass.

9. **Avoid uncomfortable situations.** Don't ask your roommate to lie for you. Don't ask your roommate to conceal illegal activity or do anything he is morally opposed to.

10. **Be a friend.** Stand by your roommate. If she is having a hard time, cheer her up. If she is happy, be happy with her. Be there for the good <u>and</u> the bad.

And, of course, a few final words from the students themselves:

**People are truly diverse in their thinking, behavior, expectations, cleanliness, desires, and world views. There are lifestyles that you would never imagine possible until you witness them under your own roof.**

RHETORIC MAJOR, KENT STATE UNIVERSITY

**Sometimes your roommate can see things about you that you can't see. Instead of getting defensive so quickly, take what he says into consideration.**

PUBLIC JUSTICE MAJOR, OSWEGO STATE UNIVERSITY

PICK YOUR BATTLES. It's not worth it to get upset over <u>everything</u>. Let some things go—or at least sleep on it and see if you are still upset in the morning.

ADVERTISING MAJOR, MICHIGAN STATE UNIVERSITY

Be graceful, forgiving, and kind. Try to support each other. Be sensitive to the fact that college is not only tough for you, but for your roommate as well.

MARKETING MAJOR, EMERSON COLLEGE

In college, we do not just grow intellectually and academically—we literally grow up. In the end, we are more independent, aware, and self-assured. I believe that confidence is molded through the roommate experience.

ENGLISH COMPOSITION MAJOR, DePAUW UNIVERSITY

*No one is the perfect roommate. Not even you.*

SOCIOLOGY MAJOR, GUSTAVUS ADOLPHUS COLLEGE

**Enjoy it! It goes by too fast!**

LAW MAJOR, ALBANY LAW SCHOOL